tribal designs for needlepoint

Australian X-ray Fish Pillow

tribal designs for needlepoint

30 ORIGINAL DESIGNS
ADAPTED FROM ESKIMO,
POLYNESIAN AND INDIAN ART

gay ann rogers

Doubleday & Company, Inc., Garden City, New York
1977

Library of Congress Cataloging in Publication Data

Rogers, Gay Ann.
Tribal designs for needlepoint.

1. Canvas embroidery—Patterns. 2. Indians
of North America—Art. 3. Art, Polynesian.
4. Designs, decorative—Themes, motives. I. Title.
TT778.C3R6   746.4'4
ISBN: 0-385-09967-3
Library of Congress Catalog Card Number 76–2814

Book design by Beverley Gallegos

9   8   7   6   5   4   3   2

For my husband, Jim, whose patience and good humor kept me going.

acknowledgments

The following friends have been of help and good cheer in the preparation of this book:

Sage Belt
Margaret Crull
Deek Kelley
Edgerton and Lily Bell Scott
Jane Stevens
Marion Stewart
Carl and Barbara Strona

I am very grateful to Kathleen Johnston for spending endless hours with me making "x's" on the graphs.

To my husband, Jim, I am indebted for all the photographs.

My special thanks go to my editor, Karen Van Westering, for excellent advice and generous assistance.

A portion of the receipts from the sale of this book will go to *Terra*, the quarterly magazine of the Natural History Museum of Los Angeles County to help diffuse knowledge about the ethnic groups whose designs appear in this book.

contents

introduction

When I first began designing needlepoint canvases, it seemed natural that I should turn to tribal motifs as a source of designs. Old as many of the motifs are, they often look contemporary, and I wanted an approach to needlepoint that was not traditional and flowery. I also wanted to use designs that enhanced the characteristics of needlepoint: the geometric quality, the jagged edges of curves, and the texture of the yarn. I sought a result that looked as though it belonged to the field of textiles rather than to the medium of painting. Tribal designs are excellent for this approach, and they translate easily and effectively into needlepoint.

During the years that I have been stitching and designing needlepoint, I have frequently heard the opinion that needlepoint would be fascinating to work if only the designs were not so traditional. I have tried to show in this book that needlepoint designs need neither traditional European tapestries nor flowery scenes as sources of inspiration.

Most of the designs in this book share a major trait, although the tribes themselves had little communication with one another. They lived in areas in or near the Pacific, ranging from the Arctic to south of the Equator, and from prehistoric times to the present. The motifs on their artifacts emphasize linear design, whether complex and detailed or bold and simple, over qualities such as color and dimensional forms. So important is linear design to the dynamic quality of most of these tribal motifs that quite often the individual figures in a given motif are not as important to the design as is the context in which they are fitted.

The individual figures in a motif are often the barest representation of plants, animals, and people. Where we might think it necessary to indicate shadows to stress the dimensions of a form, they either ignore dimensions or represent them simply in a linear form by means of small dots or lines. Nonetheless, it should be noted, that most of these tribal designs show, when the effect is desired, a detailed knowledge of the anatomy or structure of the organism they represent.

The tribes of the northwest coast of America, whose designs are both strongly detailed and highly complex, are a good example of this emphasis on linear design. The detailed faces and figures and their complex interrelation in both the Chilkat Blanket Pillow (p. 53) and the Tlingit Drum Pillow (p. 63) create a powerful design with a minimum use of color and dimensional forms.

The same approach is also apparent in a tribe as far away from the Indians of the northwest coast of America as the aborigines of Australia, who made the so-called "X-ray Paintings" on bark. In the Australian X-ray Fish Pillow (p. 45), you can see again the same emphasis on linear design rather than on many colors and dimensional forms to achieve the effect of form and space.

This emphasis on linear design is perhaps most striking in the designs from the Solomon Islands drum (p. 35) and from the Hohokan pot (p. 125). Although the first design comes from the Asian side of the Pacific and the second from the southwest area of North America, they share in common a reliance on linear design alone—in this case jagged lines around the major figures—to achieve the same dynamic effect of making the major figure appear to vibrate before our eyes.

It is interesting that the approach to design of those tribes still existing today in these regions continues along the same line. The Eskimo designs in this book, for example, are contemporary. The solution to the design problems faced by the artist remains, however, very similar to the approach of most of the tribal designs from other areas and other times. The Eskimo designs depend upon a linear quality and the interrelation of figures to achieve their impact. In both Kenojuak prints (pp. 71–75), for example, the emphasis is on the interrelation of birds and other animals around the sun portrayed by a simple but effective linear design rather than by the use of color or multidimensional effects.

The designs included here are adaptations of original tribal motifs. I have chosen those designs that translate easily into needlepoint and do not ask the impossible of canvas and yarn. I have kept the needlepoint designs as close to the original as possible, altering the linear design only to fit the mesh grid of the canvas. As far as yarn colors would permit, I have attempted to use the colors of the original design. In those designs where I felt that other colors made a better needlepoint design or were the only colors available in yarn, I have also listed the original colors.

With the graph for each design, I have included a brief history of the original tribal motif, a key for yarn colors and decorative stitches, and instructions for stitching each design. For most of the designs, I have also suggested various ways to alter them to make rugs, hangings, and other objects.

Eskimo Print Pillow of Two Quails

getting started

supplies

To stitch the designs in this book, you will need the following supplies: canvas, yarn, needles, scissors, thimble (optional), and masking tape.

Canvas

The two traditional types of canvas for needlepoint are: 1) penelope, a double-thread canvas; and 2) mono, a single-thread canvas. Penelope canvas has double threads which keep the stitches from slipping. Also, the canvas holds its shape well. Mono canvas with single threads is easier for beginners. A good grade of mono will hold its shape well. A more recent canvas called interlocking is gaining popularity. It has double threads like penelope, but they are woven to resemble the single thread of mono. The type of canvas used for most projects is a matter of personal preference.

Canvas is available in bleached (white) and unbleached (yellow, tan, brown) colors. If you can obtain it, unbleached canvas is preferable because the white canvas threads often show through dark yarn colors.

The canvas mesh size means the number of canvas threads (meshes) to the inch. It varies from 3 meshes to the inch to 54 meshes to the inch. The mesh sizes recommended for the designs in this book are 5, 8, 10, 12, 14, 16, and 18 meshes to the inch.

Yarns

Needlepoint yarns are available in an incredibly wide variety of colors. I used two high-quality yarns to stitch the examples in this book: Paterna Persian yarn and Nantucket Tapestry yarn. I use Paterna for designs stitched on 10-, 12-, and 14-mesh canvas, and Nantucket for designs stitched on 16- and 18-mesh canvas because Nantucket covers the smaller mesh canvas more completely. (See "Suppliers," p. 159.)

Other excellent yarns are available as well. Knitting yarns, however, should not be used. They are not twisted as tightly as tapestry or Persian yarns and do not have their strength. They will fray unevenly from the stress of being pulled through the canvas, and the result will be an undesirable thick and thin effect on the surface of the stitched needlepoint.

Needles

Needlepoint requires tapestry needles that have blunt ends and large holes for ease of threading. They are available in assorted sizes from number 13 (large) to number 26 (small). Use size 13 needles with 5-mesh canvas; size 16 needles with 8-mesh canvas; size 18 needles with 10-mesh canvas; size 20 needles with 12-mesh canvas; size 20 or 22 needles with 14-mesh canvas; size 22 needles with 16-mesh canvas; and size 22 or 24 needles with 18-mesh canvas.

Scissors

A good pair of sharp scissors can be a great help in stitching. If they have very sharp points, they will ease the task of ripping (removing yarn) when a mistake is made. This happens inevitably to everyone at some time. I have a tiny pair of antique Victorian scissors with points so sharp they will rip yarn from petit-point canvas with as much ease as most embroidery scissors rip yarn from 10-mesh canvas. They have become so necessary to my work that I keep them on a ribbon around my neck while I am stitching. If you tend to misplace your scissors, as I do, a ribbon or some similar attachment helps to save time and patience.

Thimble

When I am stitching I always wear a thimble. I cannot imagine being without one, but apparently not everyone finds a thimble necessary.

Masking Tape

Fold one-inch-wide masking tape over the raw edges of your canvas before beginning to work. It will keep the edges of your canvas from unraveling.

your project

Thread Count

After choosing the design you wish to stitch, your next decision is which canvas mesh to use. Your choice of mesh size will determine the size of your finished project: the smaller the canvas mesh, the smaller the finished project; the larger the canvas mesh, the larger the finished project.

I have included with the instructions for working each graph a thread count of each design. A thread count is the number of meshes that will eventually be stitched along each side of the design at its widest or longest point. For example, the thread count of the Chilkat Blanket design on page 53 is 314 threads by 314 threads.

The thread count of a graphed design is important because it remains a constant measurement, while the size of a graphed design in inches will vary according to the mesh size of the canvas. If the Chilkat Blanket design (314 threads by 314 threads) is worked on 18-mesh canvas, the finished needlepoint piece will be about 17½ inches square. If done on 5-mesh canvas, the same design will be about 63 inches square.

To find the size of any graphed design on a given canvas mesh size, you need only to follow this simple formula: divide the thread count of the design by the canvas mesh size to determine the size of the project on one side in inches. For example, the Chilkat Blanket design's thread count of 314 divided by 18 (the canvas mesh size) equals about 17½ inches. Since the Chilkat Blanket is square, both sides will be 17½ inches each.

This is a very simple formula to use, and it is very convenient if you need a finished project of a specific size. This is necessary, for example, if you want to do needlepoint upholstery. For the designs in this book, I have recommended in the instructions at least one canvas mesh size and given the dimensions in inches of the finished needlepoint piece when worked on that size canvas.

Cutting the Canvas

After you have decided which size canvas to use and determined the size of the finished design, you cut a piece of canvas equal to the dimensions of your finished project plus a minimum of 1½ inches extra on *each* side. For example, you will need a 17-inch-square piece of canvas for a 14-inch-square finished project: 1½ inches + 14 inches + 1½ inches = 17 inches. The extra one and a half inches of canvas is the *minimum* extra canvas that is necessary on each side for blocking and finishing your needlepoint project.

Bind each edge of the cut piece of canvas with masking tape to keep the canvas from unraveling. If you are working on a long-term project, you may find that cloth bias tape sewn over the edges of the canvas wears better than masking tape.

Spraying the Canvas with Acrylic Fixative

You will notice in the instructions for stitching the designs that I frequently refer to the use of pens and paints. If you use these on canvas, they must be waterproof. It is impossible to be certain, however, that supposedly waterproof inks and paints will not bleed. If they do bleed into the yarn when your piece of needlepoint is dampened for blocking, there will be no way to remove the stains from the yarns. You will have no alternative but to spend hours ripping and replacing yarn. A simple precaution will eliminate the problem of bleeding inks and paints. After you have marked your canvas with ink or paint, spray the canvas thoroughly on both sides with an acrylic fixative, which is available from most art-supply stores.

stitching

Most of the designs in this book are worked from the center of the design outward to the edges. For the few designs that are not stitched this way, detailed instructions are given with each graph.

To work from a center point, find and mark the exact center of the graphed design. You can find this center of the graph by following the arrows at the edges of the graph to the common point or points where they intersect. Where there are two arrows at each edge, double center is indicated so that decorative stitches will work out evenly on both sides of the design. Find and mark the center of your canvas with a waterproof pen to correspond to the center of the graph. At this point, in addition to marking the center it is advisable to mark the outer edges of the design also.

Each square on the graph represents one stitch on the canvas. To begin stitching, count off the squares of your design from the center and stitch each corresponding mesh of the canvas.

If you want to avoid counting off the squares of your design while stitching, you can transfer the entire design to the canvas before starting to stitch. Count off the squares of your design from the center of the graph and mark each corresponding mesh of your canvas with a waterproof pen. Use different waterproof pens to mark the boundaries where different colors meet.

The advantage of this method is that you do all your counting at one time. This can be very helpful if you plan to take your needlepoint where distractions may interrupt the concentration needed to count while stitching. This method also makes it possible to paint your canvas. Painting is not necessary, but there are good reasons for doing it. You will always know where each color goes without carrying a color key. More important, your yarn will always have the same color underneath to prevent flecks of canvas from showing through your stitched piece. Directions for painting your canvas are in the section on designing your own needlepoint.

Mirror-image Designs

For many of the designs in this book, I have graphed only one half of the design because the design is repeated in the other half as though reflected in a mirror. The term, mirror image, in the directions means a repetition in *reverse* of the graphed half of the design.

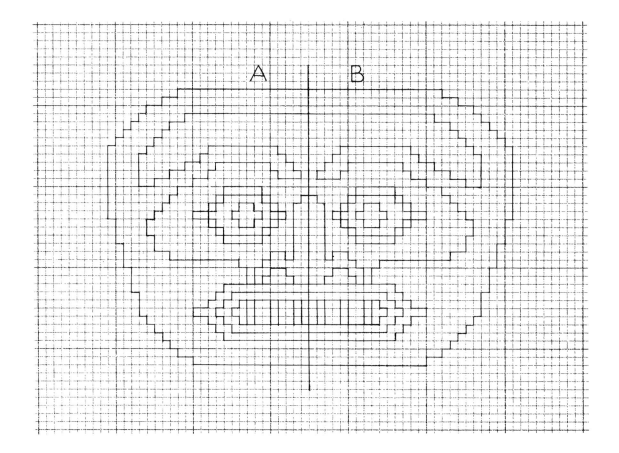

Mirror Image (A is the mirror image of B.)

Decorative Stitches

The symbols on each graph represent different colors and, in some instances, different decorative stitches. The names are given in the color and stitch key accompanying each of the graphs. At the end of the book is a glossary in alphabetical order of decorative stitch diagrams. If you are unfamiliar with the name of a certain stitch mentioned in the key of a graph, this glossary of stitch diagrams will give you the pattern for that stitch.

It is not necessary to use the decorative stitches indicated in the graphs. If you prefer, you can stitch all the designs in this book in Basketweave and Continental. By contrast, when the graph indicates only Basketweave or Continental, you may use other decorative stitches. With most of the graphs, I have suggested alternative ways of stitching the design.

Color

Each graph includes color suggestions and corresponding yarn numbers indicated on a color key. Most of these colors are as close to the original design as yarn colors permit. Do not let these original colors prevent you from trying new ones. The designs are often just as effective with other color combinations. With most of the graphs, I have suggested alternative color combinations, but do not hesitate to experiment on your own.

Hopi Kachina Pillow

the designs

hawaiian quilt pillow

This design is adapted from a Hawaiian quilt with motifs reflecting native plants and the royal Hawaiian crown. The Hawaiians learned the technique of quilting from New Englanders in the middle of the nineteenth century. The designs came, however, from their own coverlets made of white tapa cloth stenciled with red motifs. In transferring this design to the New England quilt, the Hawaiian women repeated the motifs at each corner of the quilt, and then placed a medallion in the center. Most of the motifs came from nature, a lesser number from historical themes.

Canvas

The Hawaiian quilt design measures 300 threads by 300 threads. Cut and bind a piece of 14-mesh canvas 25 inches square to obtain a finished piece about 21 inches square.

Stitching Directions

Mark the center of the canvas with an indelible marker. Follow the arrows marked at the edges of the graph to find the starting point for the graph. This point corresponds to the center of the canvas.

Begin to stitch at the center of the canvas. The quilt is a four-way design. The graph represents the lower right-hand quarter of the finished design. Stitch this first quarter, and then repeat it in a mirror image. You will now have completed half of the design. Stitch the last two quarters in mirror images of the first two.

Color and Stitch Key

The original quilt has a bright red design equivalent to Paterna ✻242 appliquéd on a white background equivalent to Paterna ✻005. I reversed the colors and stitched the design in off-white and used a dark red for the background. Yarn numbers refer to Paterna yarns. See color Plate 11.

Stitch the design in Basketweave or Continental and the background in Diagonal Mosaic. Reverse the direction of the stitches for each quarter so that the finished piece is a true four-way design.

Creative Alternatives

The example in the picture is a large floor pillow stitched on 14-mesh canvas. The design would make a smaller pillow (almost 17 inches square) if stitched on 18-mesh canvas. It would make a 37½-inch-square rug if stitched on 8-mesh canvas.

For stitching this pillow or variations on it, an alternative background stitch of either Mosaic or Cashmere would work as well. Other colors would also capture the spirit of the original design as long as they are two strongly contrasting colors, both bright or both muted.

samoan
tapa cloth pillow

This design is adapted from a Samoan tapa cloth. This "cloth" is not a woven textile but is made from beaten bark. Although tapa has been used in Asia, Africa, and South America, the best tapa came from Polynesia. The most common source of Samoan tapa was the paper mulberry which produced a creamy white-colored tapa.

After the bark was removed and the outer part scraped off, the bark was soaked for 24 hours and scraped again with a shell. The Samoan women then beat the dried strips of scraped bark with mallets to spread the bark fibers and knit them together. They joined the beaten strips with an adhesive made of boiled arrowroot.

The design pattern, usually made from coconut leaflet midribs, was covered with native dyes of brown, black, and red. The women then pressed the tapa cloth over the design pattern and placed the dyed tapa in the sun to dry. They often retouched the dyed design by hand to make it more vibrant.

Canvas

The tapa cloth pillow measures 144 threads by 144 threads. Cut and bind a piece of 10-mesh canvas 18 inches square to obtain a finished piece about 14½ inches square.

Stitching Directions

Mark the center of the canvas with an indelible marker. Follow the arrows marked at the edges of the graph to find the starting

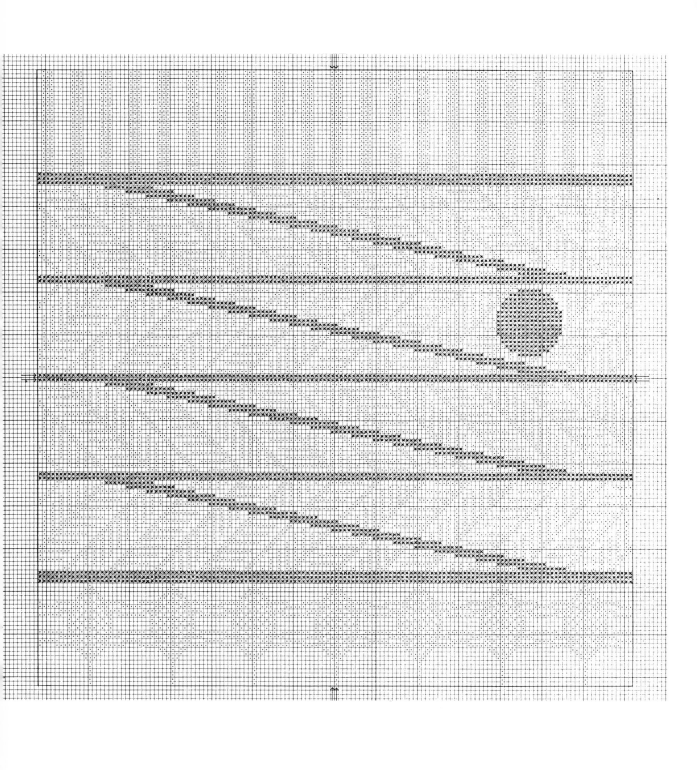

point for the graph. This point corresponds to the center of the canvas. Begin to stitch at the center of the canvas. Stitch the dark brown stripes first in Basketweave or Continental and then fill in the lighter details.

Color Key

The colors used in the tapa cloth pillow and those suggested in the color key are the colors from the original design. Yarn numbers refer to Paterna yarns. See color Plate 10.

Creative Alternatives

The tapa cloth from which I adapted this design consists of many squares of which my design is only one. By putting 8 of the squares together (2 rows of 4 squares) you can make an attractive rug similar to the original cloth. Omit the dark circle from several of the squares to give a random effect to the overall design. A rug of 8 squares requires a piece of 8-mesh canvas 39 by 75 inches or 10-mesh canvas 32 by 61 inches.

An alternative stitch for this design would be Upright Gobelin in place of Basketweave for the brown bands across the design.

Other colors could also be used with equal effect if the bands running across the design are kept much darker and more intense than the other two colors.

X BEIGE # 103   BROWN # 106

Above, Australian Shield Pillow, Australian X-ray Fish Pillow Plate 1
Below, Solomon Island Drum Pillow, Marquesas Island Carved Coconut Pincushion,
        Papuan Votive Plaque Pillow

Eskimo Print Pillow of Owl Plate 2

Eskimo Print Pillow of Two Quail   *Plate 3*

Above, Apache Basket Pillow, Navajo Crystal Rug Pillow   *Plate 4*
Below, Navajo Rug Pillow of Train, Navajo Sand-painting Pillow

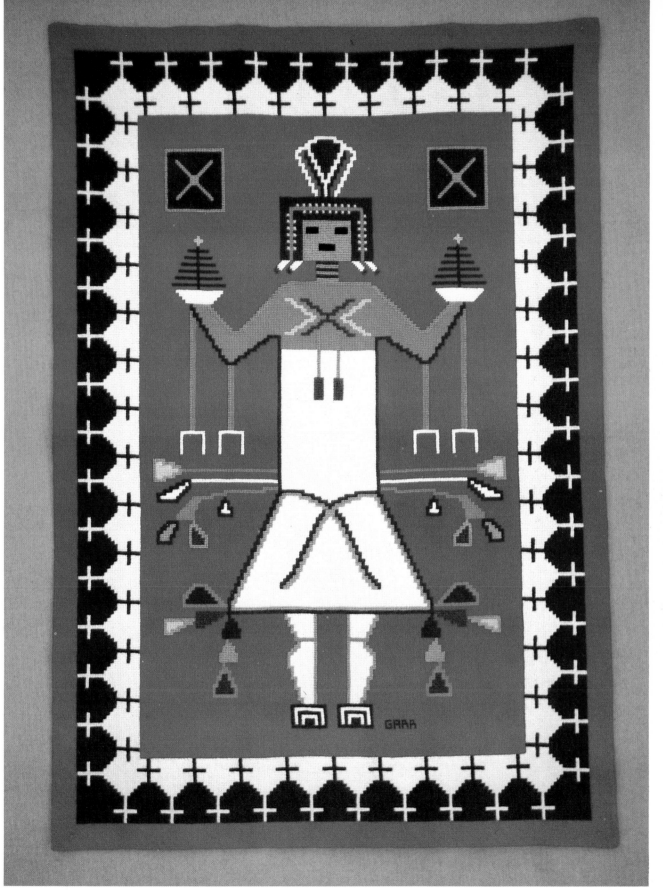

Navajo Yei Rug

Plate 5

Eskimo Print Pillows of Birds and Animals   *Plate 6*

marquesas islands carved cocoanut pincushion

This design is adapted from a carved Marquesan coconut. The Marquesans applied their designs to wood and stone carvings and to body tattooing rather than to tapa cloth.

The stylized face of this carving is typical of the Marquesan approach to design which emphasized horizontal lines. The eyes, usually carved last, are little more than geometric abstractions. The ears, as usual, are not depicted. The nose, often omitted, is here shown only as flared nostrils. The mouth has a strong horizontal line in the center of it, which probably stands for the tongue in its protruding form, a symbol of aggression. The bottom part of the coconut may be a condensed and abstract representation of the human body.

Canvas

The coconut pincushion measures 132 threads by 108 threads. Cut and bind a pice of 18-mesh canvas 11 by 9 inches to obtain a finished piece about 7½ by 6 inches.

Stitching Directions

Mark the center of the canvas with an indelible marker. Follow the arrows marked at the edges of the graph to find the starting point for the graph. This point corresponds to the center of the canvas. Begin to stitch at the center of the canvas. Stitch the design and background in Basketweave or Continental. Work all of the light-colored lines of the design first, and then fill in the darker background.

Color Key

For this pincushion, I chose a brown yarn to reflect the dark coconut, and a lighter color yarn to reflect the highlights created by the incised lines. Yarn numbers in the color key refer to Nantucket yarns. See color Plate 1.

Creative Alternatives

By using 10-mesh canvas, you could convert the pincushion into a pillow measuring about 13½ by 11 inches. This would require a piece of canvas 18 by 14 inches. The colors in the example shown in the picture could be reversed, or you could substitute other colors as long as you choose two colors with sufficient contrast to retain a very distinct design. There are so many single rows of color in this example that it would add little to the design to incorporate decorative stitches in it.

solomon islands
drum pillow

This design is adapted from a Solomon Islands drum carved of a single piece of wood. Beyond the drum proper, the wood has been carved at each end in the shape of a bird's head with a long beak diagonal to the ground. These beaks offer an easy means to carry this large drum from one ceremonial dance to another.

This drum is typical of the Solomon approach to design in its combination of human form and geometric style. The vibrant lines around each head call attention to the *mana* or spirit that, in the Solomon Islands as in Melanesia generally, was believed to reside in the human skull and be transferable from one person to another.

Canvas

The pillow measures 144 threads by 256 threads. Cut and bind a piece of 12-mesh canvas 15 by 25 inches to obtain a finished piece about 12 by 21½ inches.

Stitching Directions

Mark the center of the canvas with an indelible marker. Follow the arrows marked at the edges of the graph to find the starting point for the graph. This point corresponds to the center of the canvas. Begin to stitch at the center of the canvas.

The graph represents the right half of the finished design. Stitch the graphed half, then repeat it in a mirror image. Work the design and border first and then fill in the background.

	RUST # 414
	BASKETWEAVE OR CONTINENTAL STITCH

	OFF WHITE # 012
	MOSAIC STITCH

	BLUE # 380
	SCOTCH STITCH OVER 4 MESHES

	BLUE # 380
	BASKETWEAVE OR CONTINENTAL STITCH

Color and Stitch Key

The yarn colors shown are close to the original colors. Yarn numbers refer to Paterna yarns. In addition to Basketweave and Continental stitches, I have used Scotch and Mosaic stitches, which are indicated in the key. See color Plate 1.

Creative Alternatives

This design lends itself to several other forms. One is to stitch the design and to omit the border entirely. Another is to make a square pillow by repositioning the border around one head only (half the design) instead of around two heads. To make a pincushion, stitch one head only (half the design) on 18-mesh canvas and omit the border.

An upright Gobelin stitch could be used in place of the Scotch stitch, and a simple Cross stitch would make a good alternative to Mosaic. Avoid a large or complicated stitch for the background as it would detract from the vibrant and linear quality of the design.

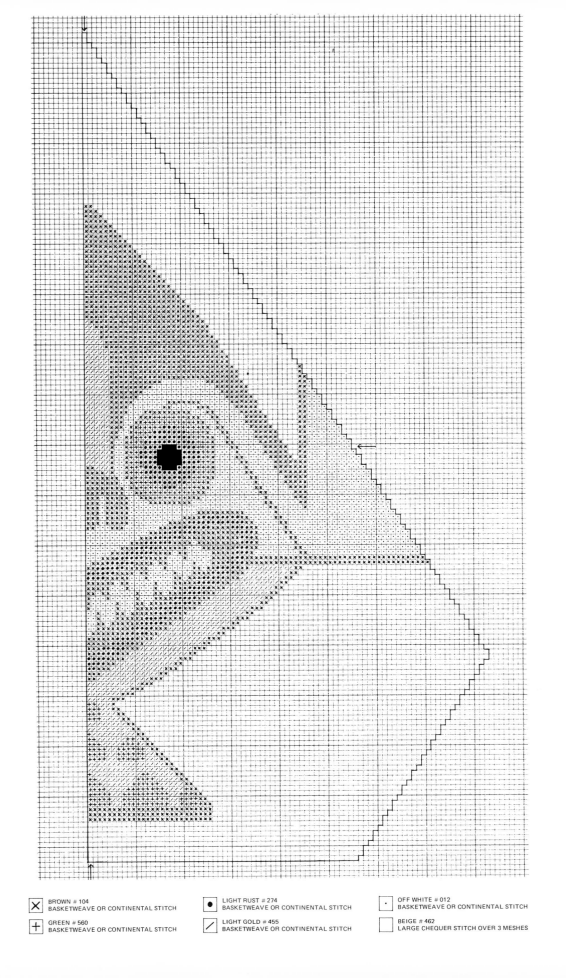

☒ BROWN # 104 BASKETWEAVE OR CONTINENTAL STITCH	● LIGHT RUST # 274 BASKETWEAVE OR CONTINENTAL STITCH	· OFF WHITE # 012 BASKETWEAVE OR CONTINENTAL STITCH
✚ GREEN # 560 BASKETWEAVE OR CONTINENTAL STITCH	╱ LIGHT GOLD # 455 BASKETWEAVE OR CONTINENTAL STITCH	☐ BEIGE # 462 LARGE CHEQUER STITCH OVER 3 MESHES

papuan votive plaque pillow

This design is adapted from a Papuan votive plaque from New Guinea. These carved and painted boards usually represent ancestors or guardian spirits. The votive plaque designs are variations on a common theme—the human face. The colors most often used are white in a lime form made from burned shells; red from burned clay; yellow from clay of that color; and black from soot or charcoal. The ingredients for the colors are mixed with water and applied to the board with a brush teased out of a mashed fibrous stick. Other colors also appear on these plaques at times. The painters are always men.

Canvas

The votive plaque pillow measures 165 threads at its highest point and 166 threads at its widest point. Cut and bind a piece of 12-mesh canvas 17 inches square to obtain a finished piece about 14 inches at its tallest and widest points.

Stitching Directions

Mark the center of the canvas with an indelible marker. Follow the arrows marked at the edges of the graph to find the starting point for the graph. This point corresponds to the center of the canvas. Begin to stitch at the center of the canvas.

The graph represents half of the finished design. Stitch the graphed half, then repeat it in a mirror image. Work the eyes, nose, and mouth first, then the face, and finally, fill in the background. I used the Large Chequer stitch for the background.

39

Color and Stitch Key

The yarn colors are as close as possible to the original painted design. Yarn numbers refer to Paterna yarns. The location and choice of other stitches are shown on the key. See color Plate 1.

Creative Alternatives

To make a square pillow out of this triangular one, extend the lines of the design at its widest points to its highest and lowest points. This would present a larger area for bolder decorative stitches. A Scotch stitch would be a good alternative for the background. To add more texture to the design, you could use Cross stitch or Mosaic stitch on the brown areas of the face. You could also change colors effectively by using beige for the face and brown for the background.

australian shield pillow

This design is adapted from an aborigine shield of Queensland in northeastern Australia. These shields were used only in war unlike other weapons, such as spears and clubs, which were also used in hunting. The aborigines' shields varied in size and type of carving or painting depending on where in Australia they came from. They were usually of wood although the aborigines carved some from thick, hard bark. Whatever the material, they always carved a handle out of the solid shield. Even the largest of these grips appears small to an American or European hand.

The shields from Queensland were usually the largest made in Australia. They were not carved on the surface as were those of some other areas. Instead, the aborigines of Queensland painted the surface in totemic patterns of various geometric designs. The color was usually a reddish-rust-ochre although they sometimes used yellow and white as well.

Canvas

The Australian shield pillow measures 130 threads by 200 threads at its widest areas. Cut and bind a piece of 12-mesh canvas 14 by 20 inches to obtain a finished piece about 11 by 17 inches.

Stitching Directions

Mark the center of the canvas with an indelible marker. Follow the arrows marked at the edges of the graph to find the starting point for the graph. This point corresponds to the center of the canvas. Begin to stitch at the center of the canvas.

The graph represents the lower right quarter of the design. Stitch this quarter, then repeat it in a mirror image. You will now

41

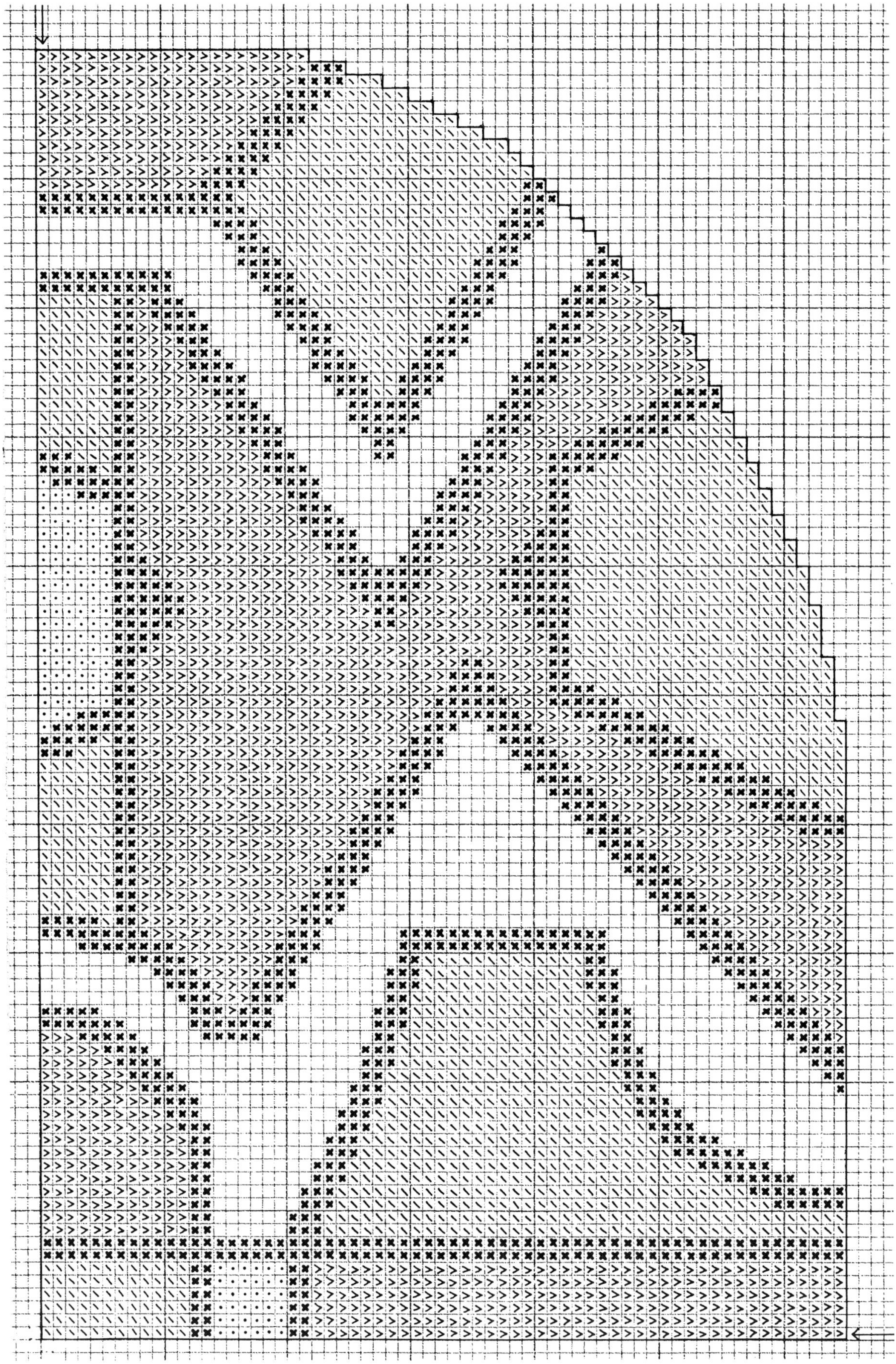

have completed half of the design. Stitch the last two quarters in mirror images to the first two.

Color and Stitch Key

The yarn colors in the color key are close to those of the original shield. Yarn numbers refer to Paterna yarns. Stitch all of the dark-brown outlines in Basketweave or Continental first, then fill in the other areas, with stitches indicated. See color Plate 1.

Creative Alternatives

This design lends itself to many different forms. To change only the color, use a dark color for the outlines and three different shades of one color in place of the rust, gold, and white, or only one shade of one color in place of those three colors. You could also use a very light color or white in place of the dark-brown outlines, and then fill in all of the other areas with dark colors.

To convert this design into a sampler, stitch the dark outlines first and then use a different stitch in each different area. This approach will be most effective if you use one color for the outlines and only one other color for all the other areas. This will emphasize the texture created by the different stitches.

To convert this oval pillow into a rectangular one, extend the lines at their widest points to the highest and lowest points of the pillow.

☒	BROWN # 110 BASKETWEAVE OR CONTINENTAL STITCH
╱	RUST # 217 HUNGARIAN STITCH
⋁	GOLD # 453 ST. GEORGE AND ST. ANDREW CROSS STITCH
•	WHITE # 005 SCOTCH STITCH OVER 3 MESHES
☐	WHITE # 005 MOSAIC STITCH

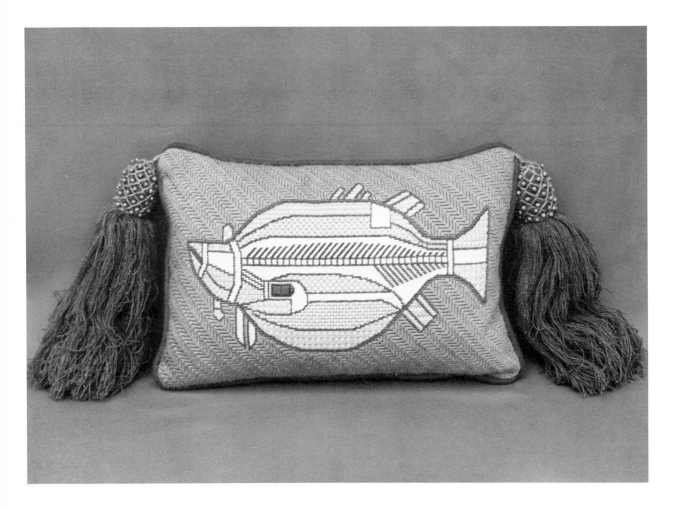

Australian X-ray Fish Pillow

australian
x-ray fish pillow

This design is adapted from an X-ray painting on bark by aborigines from Arnhem Land in northern Australia. These paintings are called "X ray" because they depict not only the external appearance of animals but also their internal skeleton and such details as the alimentary tract and eggs.

It is believed that these X-ray paintings are of extremely ancient origin. The painters depicted the animals not only as they saw them but also as they knew them, which indicates some anatomical study. The paintings were often applied to the inside surface of the bark sheets covering the shelters which the aborigines used in wet weather. Many of the paintings were associated with events from myths.

Canvas

The X-ray fish pillow measures 150 threads by 260 threads. Cut and bind a piece of 12-mesh canvas 16 by 25 inches to obtain a finished piece about 12½ by 21½ inches.

Stitching Directions

Mark the center of the canvas with an indelible marker. Follow the arrows marked at the edges of the two graphs to find the starting point for the graph. This point corresponds to the center of the canvas. Begin to stitch at the center of the canvas.

Stitch the gray and brown outlines in and around the body of the fish first. Then work all of the decorative stitch areas, and finally, do the background.

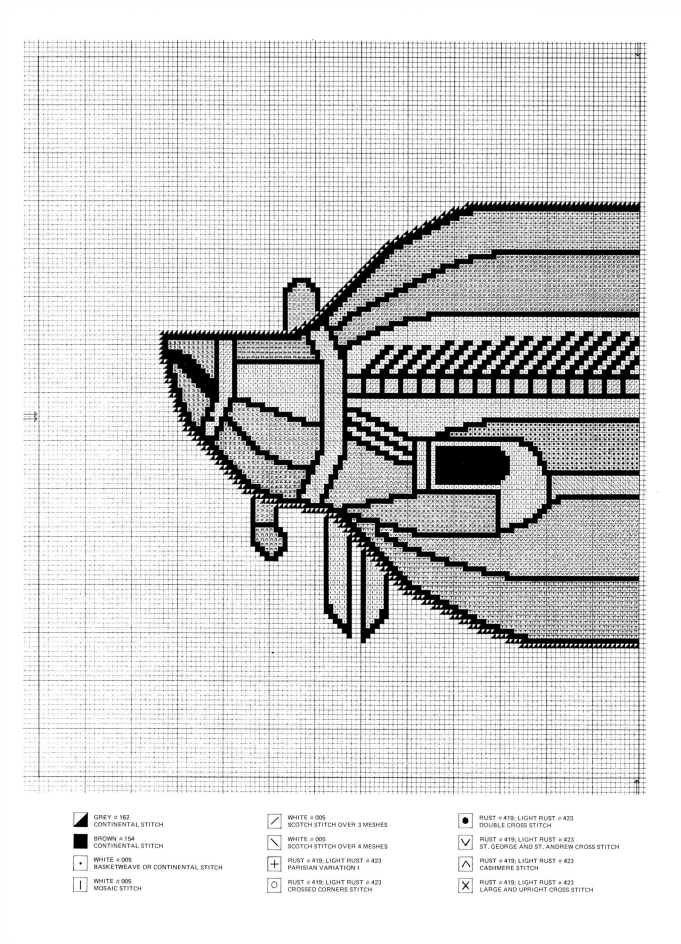

GREY # 162 CONTINENTAL STITCH	WHITE # 005 SCOTCH STITCH OVER 3 MESHES	RUST # 419; LIGHT RUST # 423 DOUBLE CROSS STITCH
BROWN # 154 CONTINENTAL STITCH	WHITE # 005 SCOTCH STITCH OVER 4 MESHES	RUST # 419; LIGHT RUST # 423 ST. GEORGE AND ST. ANDREW CROSS STITCH
WHITE # 005 BASKETWEAVE OR CONTINENTAL STITCH	RUST # 419; LIGHT RUST # 423 PARISIAN VARIATION I	RUST # 419; LIGHT RUST # 423 CASHMERE STITCH
WHITE # 005 MOSAIC STITCH	RUST # 419; LIGHT RUST # 423 CROSSED CORNERS STITCH	RUST # 419; LIGHT RUST # 423 LARGE AND UPRIGHT CROSS STITCH

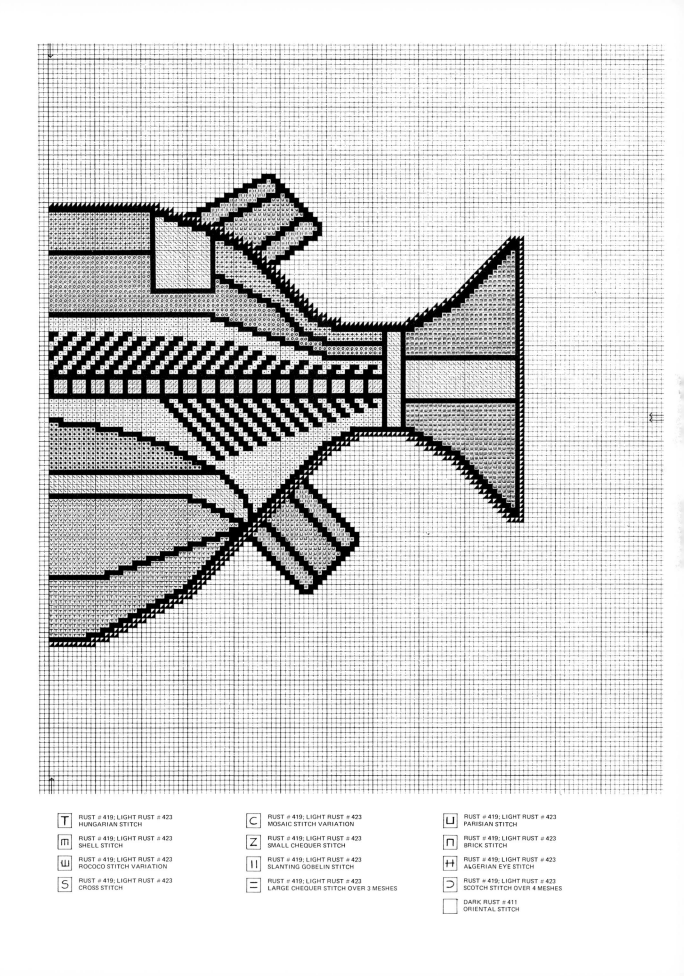

T	RUST # 419; LIGHT RUST # 423 HUNGARIAN STITCH	
m	SHELL STITCH	RUST # 419; LIGHT RUST # 423
Ш	RUST # 419; LIGHT RUST # 423 ROCOCO STITCH VARIATION	
S	RUST # 419; LIGHT RUST # 423 CROSS STITCH	

C	RUST # 419; LIGHT RUST # 423 MOSAIC STITCH VARIATION
Z	RUST # 419; LIGHT RUST # 423 SMALL CHEQUER STITCH
II	RUST # 419; LIGHT RUST # 423 SLANTING GOBELIN STITCH
=	RUST # 419; LIGHT RUST # 423 LARGE CHEQUER STITCH OVER 3 MESHES

U	RUST # 419; LIGHT RUST # 423 PARISIAN STITCH
∏	RUST # 419; LIGHT RUST # 423 BRICK STITCH
H	RUST # 419; LIGHT RUST # 423 ALGERIAN EYE STITCH
⊃	RUST # 419; LIGHT RUST # 423 SCOTCH STITCH OVER 4 MESHES
	DARK RUST # 411 ORIENTAL STITCH

Color and Stitch Key

The yarn colors in the color key are those of the original design. Yarn numbers refer to Paterna yarns. The location of the various stitches is indicated in the key. See color Plate 1.

Creative Alternatives

If you want to change the colors of this design, any four tones of a musty color plus white and gray would be effective. You could reverse the colors by using the lightest tone for the background, the two middle tones and white for the body of the fish, and the darkest tone and gray for the outlines of the fish. Another variation would be to use white for the background and all four tones of a musty color plus gray for the fish.

To change the stitches from the example used here, stitch the fish in Basketweave or Continental and use a two-tone Moorish stitch for the background.

To alter the form of the design, stitch the fish on a piece of 10-mesh canvas 13 by 24 inches to obtain a finished piece about 10 by 21 inches. Omit all of the small fins outside of the basic gray outline and do not stitch the background. Add several rows of gray around the outline of the body. Then have the fish finished as a fish-shaped pillow.

chilkat blanket belt

This design is adapted from the Chilkat blanket described on page 53.

Canvas

The graphed unit for the belt measures 32 threads by 66 threads. Cut and bind a piece of 16 mono canvas 5 inches wide and 3 inches longer than the waist measurement required. The finished piece of needlepoint will be 2 inches wide by the length of the waist measurement. If the waist measurement is 34 inches, you will need a piece of canvas 5 by 37 inches to obtain a finished piece of needlepoint 2 by 34 inches.

Stitching Directions

Mark the center of the canvas with an indelible marker. Begin to stitch at the center of the canvas. For the right half of the belt work from "A" to "B"; repeat from "A" to "B" until half the desired length is worked. For the left half of the belt work from "B" to "A"; repeat work from "B" to "A" until the desired length is completed. If you cannot stitch a full motif at the ends of the belt, omit the motif and use only the background to reach the desired length. Stitch the belt in Basketweave or Continental.

Color Key

The yarn colors in the color key are close to those in the original Chilkat blanket. Yarn numbers refer to Nantucket yarns. See color Plate 13.

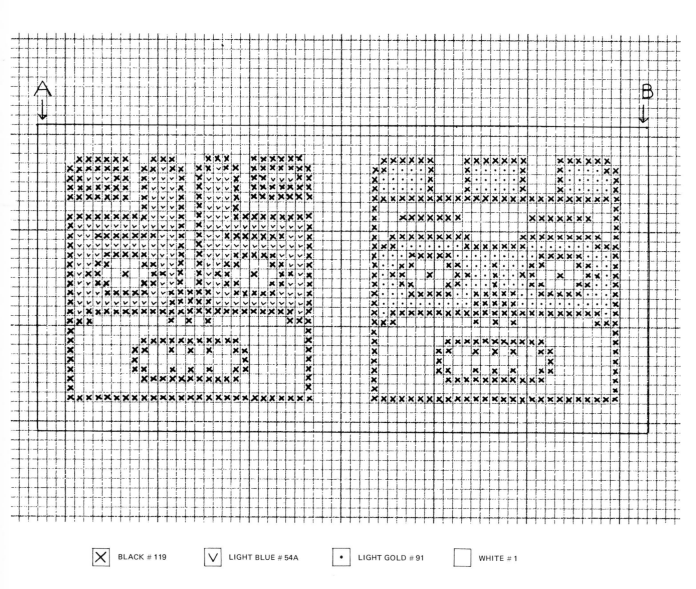

Creative Alternatives

To alter the colors, change the black to brown or dark gray, and the white to off-white. Any two soft colors could substitute for the blue and gold.

To change the stitch, you could use Brick stitch, Mosaic stitch, or Cross stitch in place of the Basketweave in the white areas.

To convert this design into a mirror or picture frame, join the belt motifs to make a border. For the top and bottom strips, use the belt motifs as they are graphed so that the heads are side by side. For the left and right strips, alter the graphed motif by dividing it in half and placing "A" on top of "B"; one head will now be on top of the other. When you finish graphing your border, you should have one head in each corner joined by a series of horizontal and vertical heads.

Chilkat Blanket Pillow

chilkat blanket pillow

This design is adapted from the central panel of a Chilkat blanket woven on the northwest coast of America. These blankets carried great prestige, and Indian tribes from Alaska to Vancouver Island wore them as ceremonial robes.

What was unique about the Chilkat blanket was not the technique of its weaving, which was traditional although complex, but the design which came from another medium—the painted board. When a Chilkat Indian wanted to design one of these blankets, he painted it first on a board. From this pattern, his wife would weave the blanket, compensating for any parts she could not reproduce in weaving by joining together separate pieces of weaving and covering the joint with white embroidery in the desired shape.

The Chilkat blanket design was highly stylized and divided into three panels separated by black and white lines. The only other colors used in the blanket were yellow and blue. The fundamental feature of the central panel was the abstract face of an animal in the center and large eyes near the top and bottom. The panels to the left and right were either abstract profiles of portions of the central face or abstract feather designs.

Canvas

The Chilkat pillow measures 314 threads by 314 threads. Cut and bind a piece of 18-mesh canvas 21 inches square to obtain a finished piece about 17½ inches square.

Stitching Directions

Mark the center of the canvas with an indelible marker. Follow the arrows marked at the edges of Graph A to find the starting

Graph A

Graph B

point for the graph. This point corresponds to the center of the canvas. Begin to stitch at the center of the canvas.

The graph represents half of the finished design. Stitch the graphed half, then repeat it in a mirror image. Work the design, background, and white portions of the border in Basketweave or Continental stitch. Then work the black and light-blue part of the border in Brick stitch.

Color Key

The yarn colors in the color key are close to those in the original Chilkat blanket. Yarn numbers refer to Nantucket yarns. See color Plate 14.

Creative Alternatives

To alter the colors, change the black to brown or dark gray, and the white to off-white. Any two soft colors could substitute for the blue and gold.

Decorative stitches would add little to this design because the interwoven faces already create such an intricate pattern. You could substitute, however, the Parisian stitch or one of its variations for the Brick stitch used in the border.

To make the pillow smaller than 17½ inches square, omit either the black or the blue portion of the border or eliminate the border entirely. To make a 16-inch-square pillow, use 14-mesh canvas and eliminate the border entirely.

If you want to convert this design into a small rug 31½ inches square, stitch the design on 10-mesh canvas.

chilkat blanket glasses case

This design is also adapted from the Chilkat blanket described on page 53.

Canvas

The glasses case measures 102 threads by 60 threads. Cut and bind 2 pieces of 16-mesh canvas 9 by 6 inches to obtain a finished piece about 6½ by 4 inches. The same design is worked on both the front and back of the case.

Stitching Directions

Mark the center of each canvas with an indelible marker. Follow the arrows marked at the edges of the graph to find the starting point for the graph. This point corresponds to the center of the canvas. Begin to stitch at the center of the canvas. Stitch the design and background in Basketweave or Continental.

Color Key

The yarn colors in the color key are close to those in the original Chilkat blanket. Yarn numbers refer to Nantucket yarns. See color Plate 13.

Creative Alternatives

To alter the colors, change the black to brown or dark gray, and the white to off-white. Any two soft colors could substitute for the blue and gold.

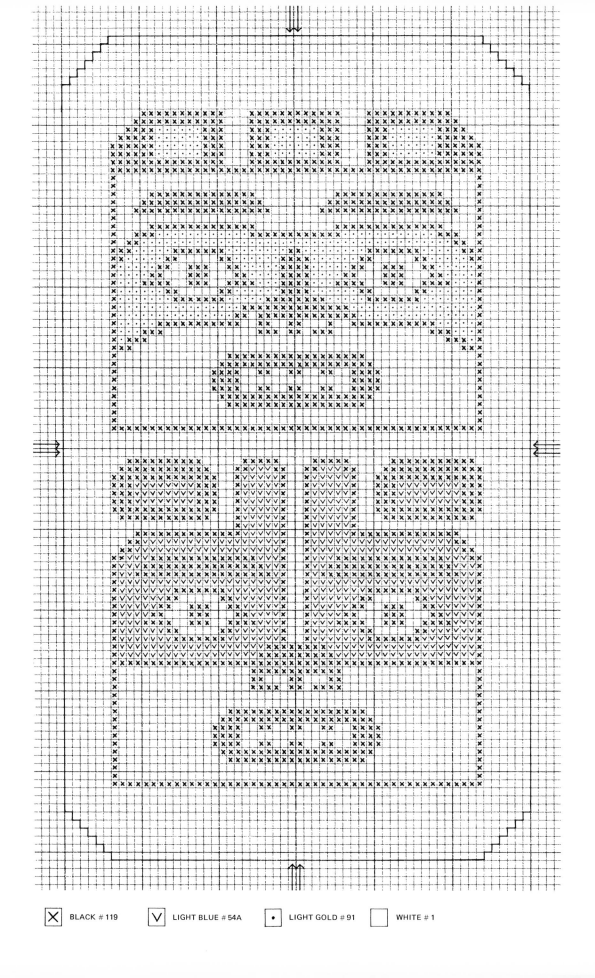

To change the stitch, you could use Brick stitch, Mosaic stitch, or Cross stitich in place of the Basketweave in the white areas.

To convert the glasses case design into a bellpull 6 by 51 inches, stitch the design on 10-mesh canvas 9 by 54 inches. Starting at the top of the graph and the top of the canvas, stitch the graphed design once. Repeat the graphed design 4 times moving down the canvas as you stitch. When you have completed the bellpull, the design will include 10 heads, one on top of another. If you want a slightly wider bellpull, add several rows of white to each edge of the design.

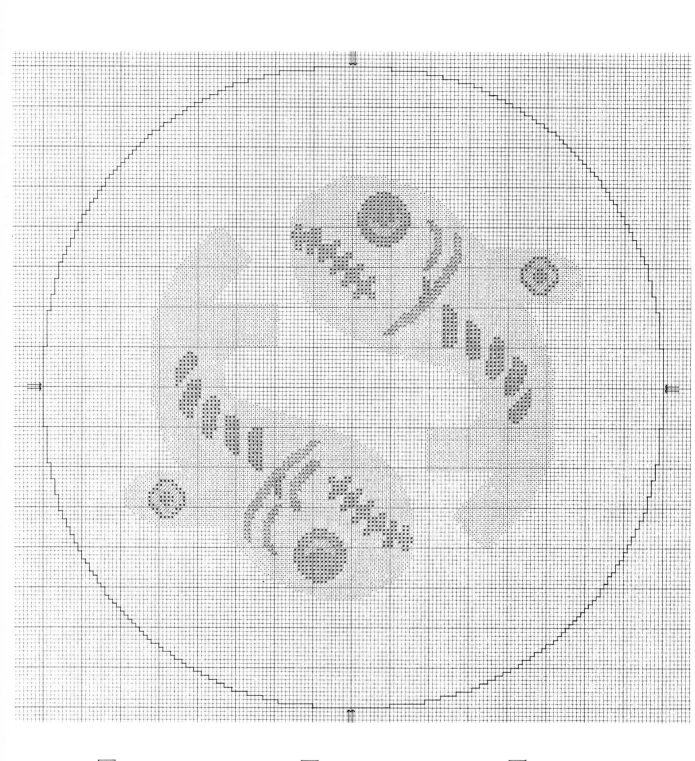

	BLACK # 108 BASKETWEAVE OR CONTINENTAL STITCH		RUST # 414 BASKETWEAVE OR CONTINENTAL STITCH		RUST # 414; LIGHT RUST # 416 DOUBLE CROSS STITCH
	WHITE # 005 BASKETWEAVE OR CONTINENTAL STITCH		LIGHT RUST # 416 BASKETWEAVE OR CONTINENTAL STITCH		

northwest tribal drum pillow

This design is adapted from an American northwest coast Indian drum. All the northwest coast Indian musical instruments were percussion type, and the drum consequently played an important role. Some drums were made out of red cedar joined like a box and painted on two sides. Others were circular and consisted of a bent-wood hoop covered with skin.

The Indians usually painted the drums with abstract figures of animals in circles regardless of the shape of the drum itself. In this example, the artist has painted the face of the drum in orange, and two killer whales in black and white in the center of the circle. The unknown Indian painter identified the whales as killer whales by the symbolic circle he painted in the dorsal fin of each whale.

Canvas

The diameter of the drum pillow measures 160 threads. Cut and bind a piece of 12-mesh canvas 17 inches square to obtain a finished piece of needlepoint about 13½ inches in diameter.

Stitching Directions

Mark the center of the canvas with an indelible marker. Follow the arrows marked at the edges of the graph to find the starting point for the graph. This point corresponds to the center of the canvas. Begin to stitch at the center of the canvas. Stitch the design first and then fill in the background.

Color and Stitch Key

The yarn colors in the color key are close to those in the original drum. Yarn numbers refer to Paterna yarns. The location and choice of stitches are indicated on the key. See color Plate 15.

Creative Alternatives

To convert the design into a small round rug 32 inches in diameter, stitch the design on 5-mesh canvas.

tlingit drum pillow

This skin drum with its black-and-red painting is typical of the skin drums used by the Tlingit Indians and their neighbors on the northwest coast of America. Actually the wooden drum was far more common on the northwest coast, and it is believed that these skin drums were obtained by trade with Indians from the interior.

What is distinctive about these skin drums is that the red-and-black designs are painted on the inside surface of the drum so that the beating of the drum will not wear away the design. Consequently, the design is visible only when the drum is placed upside down like an inverted bowl. Apparently, only the Tlingit Indians and their neighbors practiced this art of painting the underside of the drum as skin drums in other areas have their designs painted on the face side.

The design here portrays an eagle with the head in profile but the body shown from the front.

Canvas

The Tlingit drum pillow measures 184 threads by 176 threads at its widest areas. Cut and bind a piece of 12-mesh canvas 19 by 18 inches to obtain a finished piece about 15½ by 15 inches.

Stitching Directions

Mark the center of the canvas with an indelible marker. Follow the arrows marked at the edges of the graph to find the starting point of the graph. This point corresponds to the center of the canvas. Begin to stitch at the center of the canvas. Stitch the design first and then fill in the background.

	BLACK #108 BASKETWEAVE OR CONTINENTAL STITCH		WHEAT #492 BASKETWEAVE OR CONTINENTAL STITCH
	RUST #419 BASKETWEAVE OR CONTINENTAL STITCH		WHEAT #492 MILANESE STITCH

Color and Stitch Key

Camel-colored yarn represents the skin of the original drum. The black-and-red painting of the original is reproduced in black and rust yarns, Yarn numbers refer to Paterna yarns. The location and choice of stitches are indicated on the key. See color Plate 15.

Creative Alternatives

To use the original red color of the drum, substitute Paterna red ⚹240 for the rust color.

To alter the shape of the pillow, try a round or rectangular form.

In place of the Milanese stitch, try any of the following: Oriental, Moorish, Mosaic, St. George and St. Andrew Cross stitch, Parisian, or Brick.

X TURQUOISE SEED BEADS	**/** DARK GREEN SEED BEADS	**·** YELLOW SEED BEADS	OFF-WHITE # 012
V RED SEED BEADS	**●** LIGHT GREEN SEED BEADS	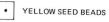 BLACK SEED BEADS	

athabascan beadwork purse

This design is adapted from a beadwork purse made by Indians of the Athabascan tribe of the Chipewyan near Lake Athabasca, Canada.

The North American Indians had long done a type of beadwork using natural materials such as shells, seeds, bones, and quills. They often dyed quills in various colors to decorate their clothes with geometric designs. With the arrival of traders in North America, the Indians soon discovered glass beads and combined them with quills and other materials. After the Indians saw floral embroidered clothes, they began to apply the beads in flowered designs as well.

Trading as well as migration was widespread among the Indians of North America, and consequently it was not uncommon to find Athabascan designs in the Southwest, nor similar designs across the continent.

Canvas

The Athabascan design measures 143 threads by 143 threads. Cut and bind a piece of 12-mesh canvas 15 inches square to obtain a finished piece of needlepoint 12 inches square.

Stitching Directions

Mark the center of the canvas with an indelible marker. Follow the arrows marked at the edges of the graph to find the starting

point for the graph. This point corresponds to the center of the canvas. Begin to stitch at the center of the canvas. Bead the design and border first and then work the background in Brick stitch.

Beading Directions

To bead this purse, you will need one 12-strand package each of turquoise, red, dark green, light green, yellow, and black opaque seed beads (for source, see "Suppliers," p. 159); one skein of embroidery floss to match each bead color; beeswax, and beading needles, which are long and thin to fit through the holes of the beads.

Be aware that these seed beads can vary in size from supplier to supplier. To determine the correct mesh-size canvas for your beads, you should make a test swatch on 12-mesh canvas. If the beads cover the canvas, and if the stitched area remains flexible so that you can bend it back and forth, then you have found the correct size canvas for your beads. If the beads do not cover the canvas, try 14-mesh canvas instead of 12 mesh. If the stitched area is stiff and inflexible, try 10-mesh canvas instead of 12.

Thread the beading needle with one ply of embroidery floss. Double the thread and coat it with beeswax for strength. You will use Continental stitch for beading. Secure the thread with two small stitches on the back. With the beading needle come up through the canvas, string one bead, and go back down through the canvas. The bead will sit on top of the canvas—representing one stitch. Repeat this process for each stitch until you have covered the design and border. Then stitch the background with yarn in Brick stitch.

Instructions for finishing the purse, making a beaded fringe, and the handle are on page 144 under "Finishing Your Project."

Color Key

The colors in the color key are close to those in the original design. Yarn numbers refer to Paterna yarns. See color Plate 12.

Creative Alternatives

Other colors would work well for this design. If you want to bead the purse, however, you will be limited by the colors available in seed beads.

Alternative stitches for the background could be the Parisian stitch or the Hungarian stitch. The background stitch should remain simple so that it does not detract from the beading.

You can convert this purse design into a pillow by stitching the design on a piece of 10-mesh canvas 17 inches square, which will give a finished piece of needlepoint about 14½ inches square. Use the following colors of Paterna yarn in place of beads: turquoise ✕755; red ✕242; dark green ✕507; light green ✕542; yellow ✕422; black ✕050.

Eskimo Print Pillow of Birds

eskimo print pillow of birds

This design and the ones following are adapted from an Eskimo stone-cut print made in Cape Dorset on West Baffin Island in the Canadian Eastern Arctic.

James Houston introduced the art of printmaking to the Eskimos of Cape Dorset in the winter of 1957. The Eskimos had incised engravings on walrus tusks for centuries, but it was not until 1957 that they learned that ink and paper made it possible to take reversed images from their walrus engravings. From that lesson, it was only a short step to the creation and use of carved printing blocks. The Eskimos chose for a carving stone a magnesium mineral called serpentine, which has a translucent and rich green color. It was an excellent choice for printing blocks as it is plentiful in the area and hard enough to take the necessary polish.

The carvers cut and polished the stone to the design of the Eskimo artist. Then Eskimo printers applied oil-based colors to the exposed and polished surface of the stone. Next, they placed the face of the paper on the inked stone and with their fingers began to rub it gently until the desired effect was achieved.

The majority of prints reflect the religion of Shamanism, a spirit world in which the Eskimo lived. Other prints drew their subject matter from nature, particularly the relation between hunter and prey, as well as from ancient legends.

This design is adapted from a 1962 stone-cut print by Kenojuak called "Arrival of the Sun." Her continuous and unbroken pattern of figures reflects the influence of earlier designs made of stencils from an elaborate web of animal skin.

Canvas

The Eskimo pillow measures 180 threads by 220 threads. **Cut** and bind a piece of 14-mesh canvas 16 by 19 inches to obtain a piece of finished needlepoint about 13 by 16 inches.

Stitching Directions

Mark the center of the canvas with an indelible marker. Follow the arrows marked at the edges of the graph to find the starting point for the graph. This point corresponds to the center of the canvas. Begin to stitch at the center of the canvas. Stitch the design first in Basketweave or Continental stitch and then fill in the background with Moorish stitch.

Color Key

The colors in the color key are close to those in the original design. Yarn numbers refer to Paterna yarns. See color Plate 6.

Creative Alternatives

To alter the colors, change the black to any of the following: brown, gray, dark blue, or musty green. Change the yellow to any of the following: rust, gold, orange, or red.

Other background stitches you might consider using in place of Moorish stitch include Diagonal Mosaic stitch, Oriental stitch, Crossed Corners stitch, or Large and Upright Cross stitch.

The shape of this pillow could be changed from a rectangular to an oval shape and would be just as attractive.

  BLACK # 108   GOLD # 440   WHITE # 005

eskimo print pillow
of animals

This design is adapted from a 1961 stone-cut print by Kenojuak called "Return of the Sun." Its similarity in design and motif to her print of birds called, "Arrival of the Sun," is immediately recognizable. Despite this similarity, the complex approach to the design of each makes them unique and yet links them as variations on the same theme.

Canvas

The pillow measures 180 threads by 220 threads. Cut and bind a piece of 14-mesh canvas 16 by 19 inches to obtain a piece of finished needlepoint about 13 by 16 inches.

Stitching Directions

Mark the center of the canvas with an indelible marker. Follow the arrows marked at the edges of the graph to find the starting point for the graph. This point corresponds to the center of the canvas. Begin to stitch at the center of the canvas. Stitch the design first in Basketweave or Continental and then fill in the background with Diagonal Mosaic stitch.

Color Key

The colors in the color key are close to those in the original design. Yarn numbers refer to Paterna yarns. See color Plate 6.

|X| BLACK # 108 |/| RUST # 225 | | WHITE # 005

Creative Alternatives

To alter the colors, change the black to any of the following: brown, gray, dark blue, or musty green. Change the rust to any of the following: gold, orange, yellow, or red.

Other background stitches you might consider using in place of Diagonal Mosaic stitch include Moorish stitch, Oriental stitch, Crossed Corners stitch, or Large and Upright Cross stitch.

The shape of this pillow could be changed from a rectangular to an oval and be just as attractive.

eskimo print pillow of two quail

This design is adapted from a stone-cut print by Kovinatilliak called "Birds of My Dreams." Despite the title, the solidity of the forms makes them appear far less ethereal and dreamlike than the prints by Kenojuak.

Canvas

The pillow measures 140 threads by 180 threads. Cut and bind a piece of 12-mesh canvas 15 by 18 inches to obtain a piece of finished needlepoint about 12 by 15 inches.

Stitching Directions

Mark the center of the canvas with an indelible marker. Follow the arrows marked at the edges of the graph to find the starting point for the graph. This point corresponds to the center of the canvas. Begin to stitch at the center of the canvas. Stitch the design first in Basketweave or Continental and then fill in the background with Brick stitch.

Color Key

The colors in the color key are close to those in the original design. Yarn numbers refer to Paterna yarns. See color Plate 3.

Creative Alternatives

Some other equally attractive color combinations would be the following: black to brown, rust to camel, with a pale-beige background; black to gray, rust to gold, with a very pale-gray background; black to musty green, rust to gold, with an off-white background; black to musty blue, retain the rust, with an off-white background.

Other background stitches you might consider using in place of Brick stitch include Moorish stitch, Parisian stitch, and Hungarian stitch.

To convert the pillow into a pincushion, stitch one quail on 18-mesh canvas. Fill in the background to make a rectangular shape. Omit the border stripe.

☒ BLACK # 108	▪ RUST # 414	☐ PALE GREY # 186

Navajo Two Gray Hills Rug

Plate 7

Hopi Kachina Pillow

Plate 8

Hopi Ceremonial Sash Bellpull
Hopi Ceremonial Blanket Hanging

Plate 9

Above, Mimbres Pottery Pillow, Samoan Tapa Cloth Pillow   *Plate 10*
Below,   Hohokam Pottery Pillow of Mother and Baby, Hohokam Pottery Pillow of Bug

eskimo print pillow of owl

This design is adapted from a stone-cut print by Eliyah called "Bird of Spring." The fine lines of the wings suggest the skills attained by the Eskimo carvers in the art of engraving on serpentine stone.

Canvas

The pillow measures 184 threads by 208 threads. Cut and bind a piece of 14-mesh canvas 17 by 18 inches to obtain a piece of finished needlepoint about 13 by 15 inches.

Stitching Directions

Mark the center of the canvas with an indelible marker. Follow the arrows marked at the edges of the graph to find the starting point for the graph. This point corresponds to the center of the canvas. Begin to stitch at the center of the canvas. Stitch the design first and then fill in the background.

Color and Stitch Key

The yarn colors are close to those of the original design. Yarn numbers refer to Paterna yarns. The location and choice of stitches are indicated on the key. See color Plate 2.

 BLACK #108
BASKETWEAVE OR CONTINENTAL STITCH

RUST #247
BASKETWEAVE OR CONTINENTAL STITCH

BROWN #154
BASKETWEAVE OR CONTINENTAL STITCH

GREEN #590
BASKETWEAVE OR CONTINENTAL STITCH

 GOLD #445
BASKETWEAVE OR CONTINENTAL STITCH

GRAY #162
BASKETWEAVE OR CONTINENTAL STITCH

WHITE #005
BASKETWEAVE OR CONTINENTAL STITCH

WHITE #005
BRICK STITCH

Creative Alternatives

You might like to try brighter colors with this design: use bright green and gold and substitute bright orange for brown and rust. You could also stitch the owl in four or five tones of the same color. A musty blue would make the owl look very eerie. You could reverse the colors by stitching the owl in white and using brown or green in place of the white background and the white areas of the owl.

In place of the Brick stitch, try any of the following: Oriental, Milanese, Large and Upright Cross stitch, and Parisian.

navajo rug pillow of train

This design is adapted from an early twentieth-century Navajo rug. The Navajo Indians learned to weave in the seventeenth century from the Pueblo Indians of the Southwest.

The Navajo rug has a distinctive character that makes it generally identifiable. The Navajo woman usually weaves a geometric design from a pattern that exists only in her mind unless she is producing for a specific buyer. There is little symbolism in Navajo rugs, although geometric and realistic motifs may have meaning if used in the proper context. Navajo rugs usually contain a few flaws both because they are handwoven and because of a cultural tabu against producing a "perfect" rug.

Each reservation area of Arizona and New Mexico produces rugs of distinctive style and pattern although borrowing and overlapping are not unknown.

This train design may have come from the Lukachukai area of northeastern Arizona which specialized in pictorial rugs.

Canvas

The pillow measures 134 by 224 threads. Cut and bind a piece of 14-mesh canvas 13 by 19 inches to obtain a piece of finished needlepoint about 9½ by 16 inches.

Stitching Directions

Mark the center of the canvas with an indelible marker. Follow the arrows marked at the edges of the graph to find the starting point for the graph. This point corresponds to the center of the

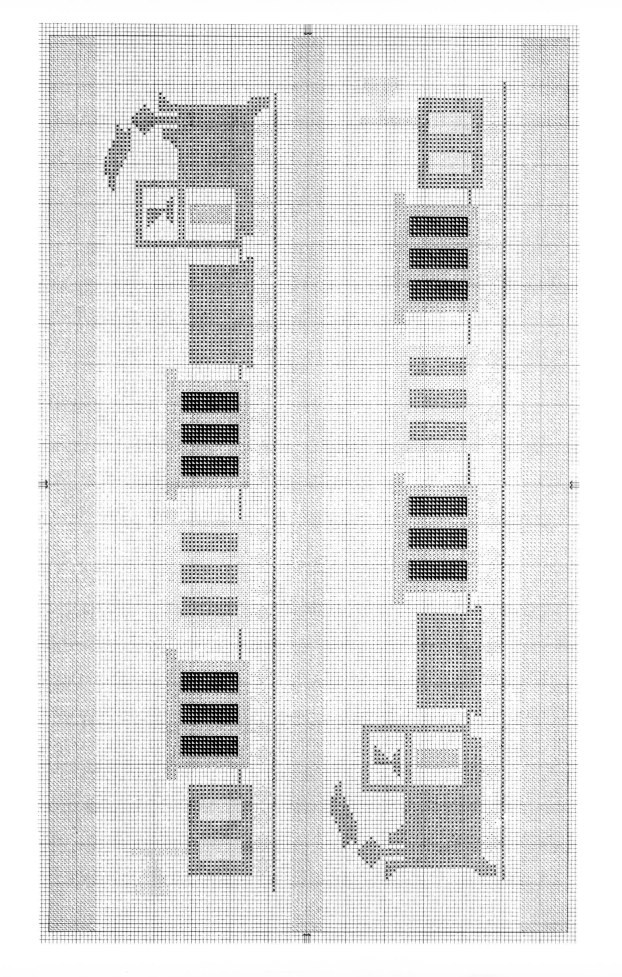

canvas. Begin to stitch at the center of the canvas. Stitch the design first and then fill in the background.

Color and Stitch Key

The colors in the color key are those of the original rug. Yarn numbers refer to Paterna yarns. The location and choice of stitches are indicated on the key. See color Plate 4.

Creative Alternatives

To alter the color, change the red background to rust, musty blue, or gold.

To change the stitch, use Cashmere stitch for the background, and for the white stripes use one of the following: Scotch stitch, Crossed Corners stitch, or Large and Upright Cross stitch.

To convert this pillow into a rug pattern very close to the original Navajo rug, cut and bind a piece of 10-mesh canvas 26 by 57 inches to obtain a piece of finished needlepoint about 22½ by 53½ inches. Starting at the top of the graph and the top of the canvas, stitch the graph design once. Repeat the graph 3 times more, moving down the canvas as you stitch. This will give you a completed rug with a design which includes 8 trains, one above the other in opposite directions, separated by white stripes.

☒	BROWN # 144 BASKETWEAVE OR CONTINENTAL STITCH
☑	ORANGE # 424 BASKETWEAVE OR CONTINENTAL STITCH
◤	GREEN # 553 BASKETWEAVE OR CONTINENTAL STITCH

•	WHITE # 005 BASKETWEAVE OR CONTINENTAL STITCH
╱	WHITE # 005 ALGERIAN EYE STITCH
☐	RED # 240 BASKETWEAVE OR CONTINENTAL STITCH

Navajo Yei Rug

navajo yei rug

This design is adapted from the Navajo Yei rug. These rugs first appeared about the turn of the century in the San Juan region of northwestern New Mexico.

Yei rugs at first caused a scandal among the Navajos, who considered it a sacrilege to depict a Navajo deity in their weaving. Collectors paid unusually high prices for such rugs, however, and they eventually became numerous in a slightly different form. The weavers generally portray in the Yei rugs participants of the Feather Dance, a part of the sacred ceremony called the Night Chant. The weavers thus avoid personifying actual Navajo deities or the use of sacred symbols by representing instead merely the dancing impersonators of the deity.

Canvas

The rug measures 340 threads by 480 threads. Cut and bind a piece of 10-mesh canvas 37 by 51 inches to obtain a piece of finished needlepoint 34 by 48 inches.

Stitching Directions

Mark the center of the canvas with an indelible marker. Follow the arrows marked at the edges of the graph to find the starting point for the graph. The graph for the rug represents half of the finished design. The graph itself is divided into 3 sections—A, B, and C. Stitch the graphed half and then repeat it in a mirror image to complete the design. Stitch the design, border, and background in Basketweave.

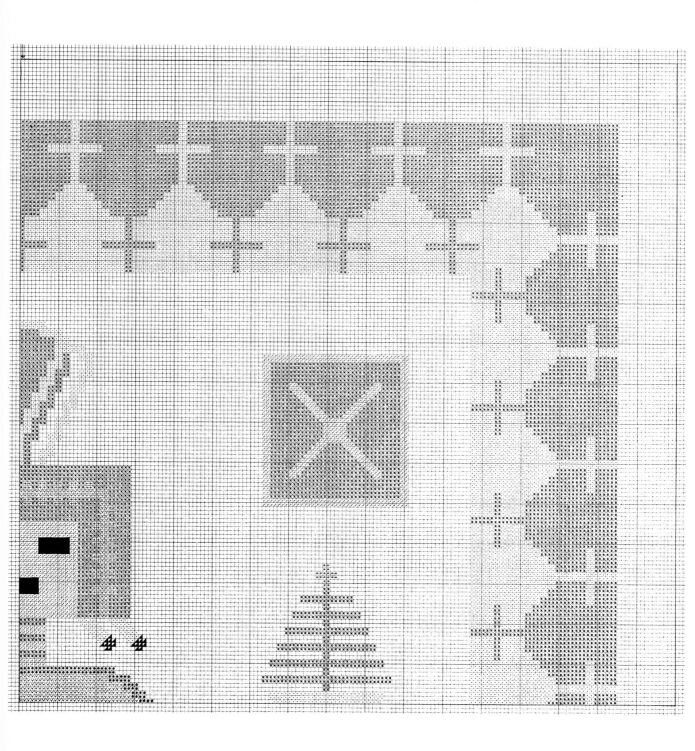

Graph A

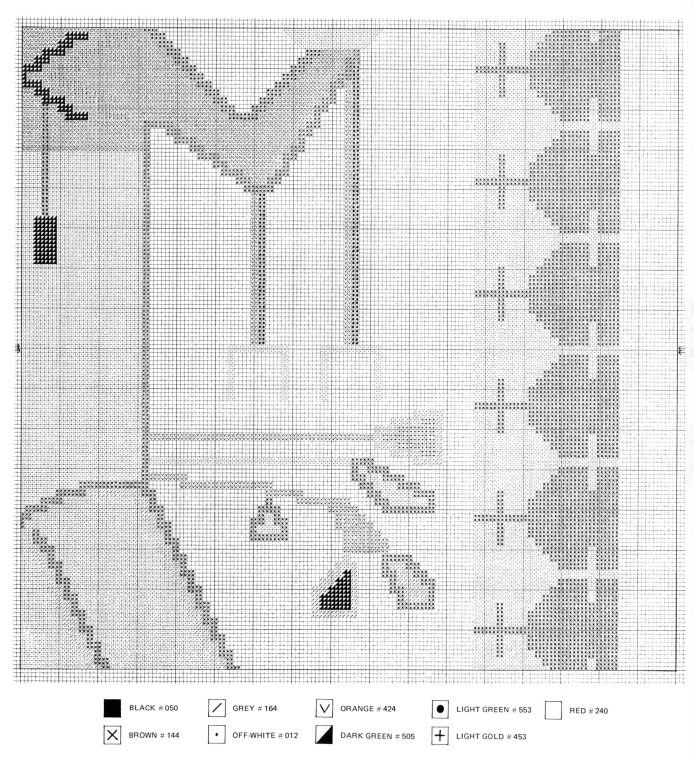

■ BLACK # 050	╱ GREY # 164	∨ ORANGE # 424
⊠ BROWN # 144	· OFF-WHITE # 012	◣ DARK GREEN # 505

● LIGHT GREEN # 553	▢ RED # 240
✚ LIGHT GOLD # 453	

Graph B

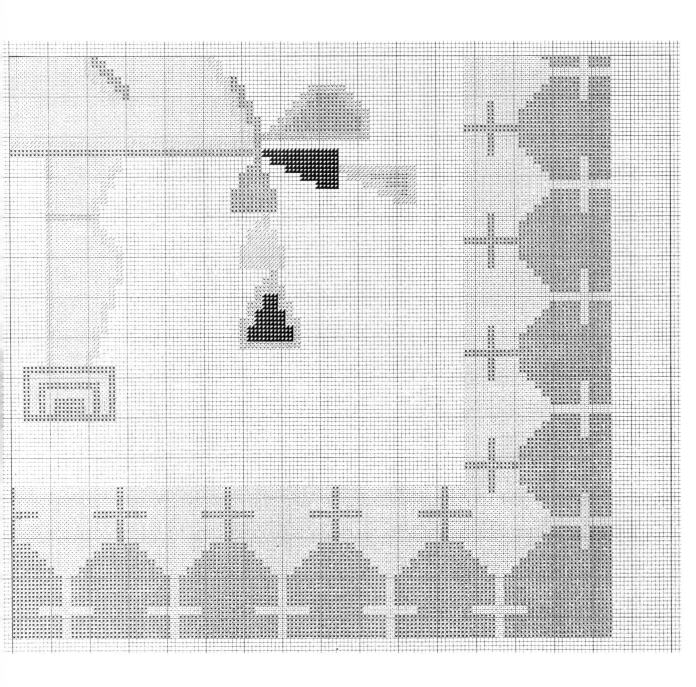

Graph C

Color Key

The colors in the color key are close to those of the original rug. Yarn numbers refer to Paterna yarns. See color Plate 5.

Creative Alternatives

To alter the colors, use a rust, camel, or gold in place of the red.

Do not change the stitch if you plan to use the rug on the floor. I have stitched the rug entirely in Basketweave because it will wear better and not snag.

To increase the size of the rug to about 42½ by 60 inches, use 8- rather than 10-mesh canvas.

Navajo Two Gray Hills Rug

navajo
two gray hills rug

This design is adapted from a Navajo rug style called Two Gray Hills which originated in northwestern New Mexico. The Two Gray Hills rug is woven of natural colors: black, white, gray, and brown.

Although design patterns vary, the basic pattern consists of geometric groupings of many small elements combined to produce a balanced and symmetrical design with one or two central motifs. These decorative elements often include triangles, stars, diamonds, and various types of diagonal bands. The rug usually has a black border and sometimes borders within borders.

Many specialists in Navajo weaving consider the Two Gray Hills rug the finest of Navajo rugs because of the high quality of its design, natural materials, and weaving. The handspun weft threads are so fine that in the work of the finest weavers they may number more than a hundred threads to an inch. The yarn is carefully spun and woven so that the rug is firm and yet soft as cashmere. In price, the best Two Gray Hills rugs compare with the highest quality Persian carpets.

Canvas

The rug measures 370 threads by 494 threads. Cut and bind a piece of 10-mesh canvas 40 by 53 inches to obtain a piece of finished needlepoint about 37 by 49½ inches.

Stitching Directions

Mark the center of the canvas with an indelible marker. Follow the arrows marked at the edges of the graph to find the starting

Graph A

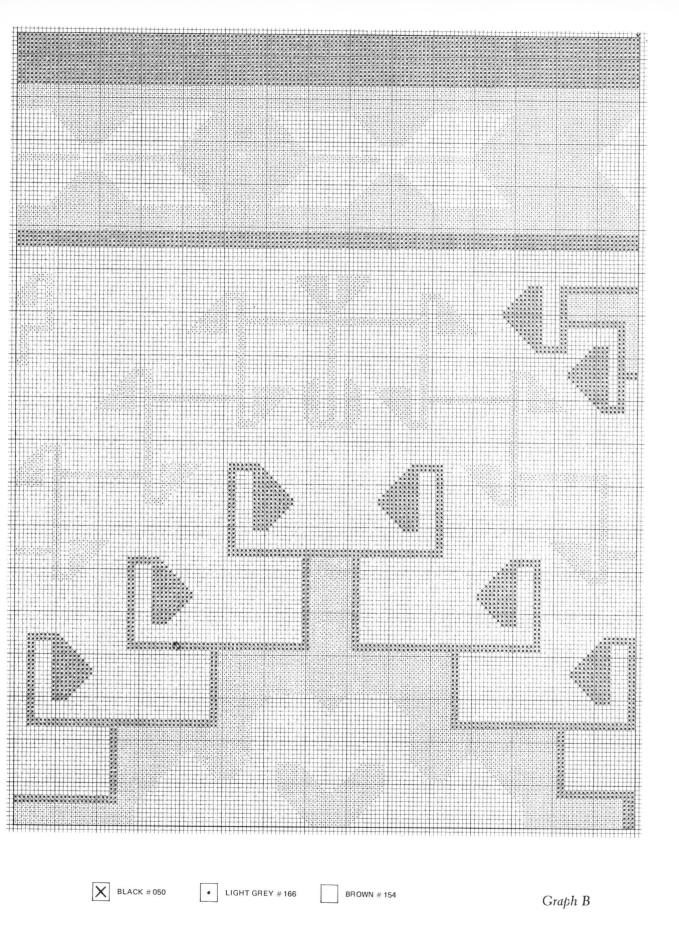

Graph B

point for the graph. This point corresponds to the center of the canvas. The graph for the rug represents one quarter of the design. Stitch this quarter, then repeat it in a mirror image. You will now have completed half of the design. Stitch the last two quarters in mirror images to the first two quarters. Stitch the design border and background in Basketweave.

Color Key

The colors in the color key are the traditional ones for this type of rug. Yarn numbers refer to Paterna yarns. See color Plate 7.

Creative Alternatives

To alter the color pattern, retain the black, but change gray areas to brown and brown areas to gray. This will give you a rug with a brown border and a gray background. To alter the colors themselves, change the brown areas to one of the following: muted blue, green, or rust.

Do not change the stitch if you plan to use the rug on the floor. I have stitched the rug entirely in Basketweave because it will wear well and not snag.

To increase the size of the rug to about 46½ by 62 inches, use 8- rather than 10-mesh canvas.

navajo crystal rug pillow

This design is adapted from a Navajo rug known as Crystal and produced in western New Mexico. The contemporary Crystal rugs are usually woven of handspun and vegetal dyed yarns. The basic pattern emphasizes horizontal bands interspersed with narrow or wavy stripes, or with wider bands consisting of various decorative geometric elements.

The contemporary Crystal rug came into existence after World War Two. Between the two World Wars, the weaving of the old-style Crystal rug, which had included red and blue colors as well as borders, gradually disappeared.

Canvas

This pillow measures 145 threads by 144 threads. Cut and bind a piece of 10-mesh canvas 18 inches square to obtain a piece of finished needlepoint about 14½ inches square.

Stitching Directions

Mark the center of the canvas with an indelible marker. Follow the arrows marked at the edges of the graph to find the starting point for the graph. This point corresponds to the center of the canvas. The graph for the pillow represents one half of the finished design. Stitch the graphed half and then repeat it in a mirror image to complete the design.

Color and Stitch Key

The colors in the color key are close to those of the original rug. Yarn numbers refer to Paterna yarns. The location and choice of stitches are indicated on the key. See color Plate 4.

Creative Alternatives

Different color combinations would also be effective in this sampler. Try black, brown, musty blue, and off-white; or charcoal gray, rust, green, and off-white.

This pillow is made as a sampler. Try a different stitch for each stripe.

To change the design of the pillow, stitch only the graphed half of the center motif. Then stitch each stripe so that it is a four-sided border around the single center motif.

To convert this pillow into a rug similar to the original, cut and bind a piece of 10-mesh canvas 32 by 47 inches to obtain a piece of finished needlepoint about 29 by 44 inches. Stitch 6 complete designs in 3 horizontal panels of 2 designs each. If you plan to use the rug on the floor rather than as a wall hanging, use only Basketweave stitch as it will wear better than others and will not snag.

BLACK # 050
BASKETWEAVE OR CONTINENTAL STITCH

BLACK # 050
MOSAIC STITCH

X BROWN # 405
BASKETWEAVE OR CONTINENTAL STITCH

● BROWN # 405
LARGE CHEQUER STITCH OVER 4 MESHES

/ GOLD # 453
UPRIGHT GOBELIN STITCH

· GOLD # 453
ALGERIAN EYE STITCH

V DARK GREY # 162
PARISIAN STITCH VARIATION II

+ GREY # 164; LIGHT GREY # 166
LARGE AND UPRIGHT CROSS STITCH

WHITE # 005
BASKETWEAVE OR CONTINENTAL STITCH

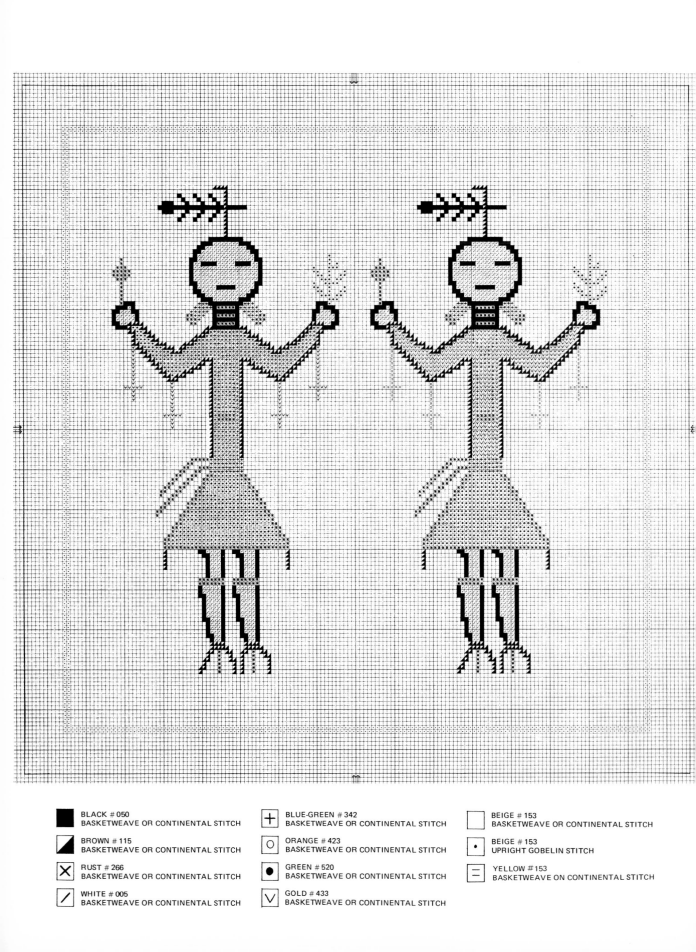

■ **BLACK # 050** BASKETWEAVE OR CONTINENTAL STITCH	✚ **BLUE-GREEN # 342** BASKETWEAVE OR CONTINENTAL STITCH	□ **BEIGE # 153** BASKETWEAVE OR CONTINENTAL STITCH
◩ **BROWN # 115** BASKETWEAVE OR CONTINENTAL STITCH	○ **ORANGE # 423** BASKETWEAVE OR CONTINENTAL STITCH	· **BEIGE # 153** UPRIGHT GOBELIN STITCH
✕ **RUST # 266** BASKETWEAVE OR CONTINENTAL STITCH	● **GREEN # 520** BASKETWEAVE OR CONTINENTAL STITCH	─ **YELLOW #153** BASKETWEAVE ON CONTINENTAL STITCH
╱ **WHITE # 005** BASKETWEAVE OR CONTINENTAL STITCH	⋁ **GOLD # 433** BASKETWEAVE OR CONTINENTAL STITCH	

navajo
sand-painting pillow

This design is adapted from a Navajo sand painting and should not be confused with a Yei rug which it may seem to resemble at first glance. Sand-painting rugs are copies of Navajo sand paintings and were first woven after World War One in the San Juan region of northwestern New Mexico.

Sand painting is a sacred ceremony among the Navajos complete with ritual and chanting to express their reverence for the creation of the world and their relation to nature. The square sand painting is created of colored sands, used ceremonially, and destroyed within twelve hours. The sand painting as a rug consequently has no meaning for traditional Navajo culture and is woven only for sale to outsiders.

As in the Yei rugs, the weavers usually omit sacred symbols and figures from the sand-painting rug. These rugs have become very popular among collectors because they represent in a permanent form the vibrant but ephemeral sand paintings of the Navajos.

Canvas

The pillow measures 172 threads by 172 threads. Cut and bind a piece of 12-mesh canvas 18 inches square to obtain a piece of finished needlepoint about 14½ inches square.

Stitching Directions

Mark the center of the canvas with an indelible marker. Follow the arrows marked at the edges of the graph to find the starting point for the graph. This point corresponds to the center of the

canvas. Begin to stitch at the center of the canvas. Stitch the design first and then fill in the background.

Color and Stitch Key

The colors in the color key are close to those of the original sand painting. Yarn numbers refer to Paterna yarns. The location and choice of stitches are indicated on the key. See color Plate 4.

Creative Alternatives

As an alternative color pattern, stitch both figures in identical colors. For a different background color, try pale gray-green, pale rust, or pale gray.

To change the background stitch, try rows of Upright Gobelin, Slanting Gobelin, Brick stitch, Parisian stitch, or Hungarian stitch. Then change the border to Cross stitch or Mosaic stitch.

To add a border to the pillow, change the color of the stripe of Upright Gobelin to black or brown. Outside the stripe of Upright Gobelin change the background color to blue-green, green, rust, or gold, and use St. George and St. Andrew Cross stitch.

To make a smaller pillow, stitch only one figure (instead of two) and use 10-mesh canvas instead of 12.

To make a larger rectangular pillow, add one or more figures in a line with the first two. Use 14-mesh canvas instead of 12.

hopi ceremonial sash bellpull

A Hopi embroidered cotton sash worn by dancers in various kachina ceremonies was the inspiration for this design. An example can be seen on the left shoulder of the Butterfly Kachina Maiden on page 110. In this needlepoint adaptation, sleigh bells, which the kachina dancers wear attached to one leg below the knee, have been added to the bellpull.

The Hopi Indians today supply many of the other pueblo tribes with their ceremonial garments which are usually made of cotton decorated with wool yarn. By contrast with the Navajos, it is the Hopi men rather than the women who are the weavers.

Canvas

The bellpull measures 513 by 80 threads. Cut and bind a piece of 10-mesh canvas 55 by 11 inches to obtain a piece of needlepoint about 52 by 8 inches.

Stitching Directions

To stitch the bellpull, start at the top of your canvas. Begin at "A" on the graph and work to "B." Then work from "C" to "D." Repeat graph from "C" to "D" 6 times more for a total of seven motifs. Then work from "E" to "F." Work the design in Basketweave or Continental stitch.

Color Key

The colors in the color key are those of the original sash. Yarn numbers refer to Paterna yarns. See color Plate 9.

| $\boxed{\text{V}}$ | GREEN # G28 | $\boxed{\text{X}}$ | RED # 240 | $\boxed{\cdot}$ | OFF-WHITE # 012 | $\boxed{}$ | BLACK # 050 |

Creative Alternatives

To alter the colors, change the green to gray (※164), the red to brown (※144), the white to black (※005), and the black to white (※012).

To add decorative stitches, use Upright Gobelin stitch for all white areas, Basketweave or Continental stitch for all red areas, Brick stitch for all green areas, and St. George and St. Andrew Cross stitch for all black areas.

To shorten the bellpull, work from "C" to "D" fewer times; to lengthen, work from "C" to "D" more times. To convert the design to a pincushion, stitch on a piece of 18-mesh canvas from "A" to "F" once for a single motif pincushion about 5½ by 4½ inches in size.

A

B
C

D
E

F
G

H

| | BLACK # 050
BASKETWEAVE OR CONTINENTAL STITCH | | BROWN # 405
MOSAIC STITCH | | BROWN # 405
BASKETWEAVE OR CONTINENTAL STITCH | | OFF-WHITE # 012
BASKETWEAVE OR CONTINENTAL STITCH |

hopi ceremonial blanket hanging

This design is adapted from a rare Hopi ceremonial blanket made in the early nineteenth century of white cotton with the design embroidered by hand.

Canvas

The wall hanging measures 388 threads by 108 threads. Cut and bind a piece of 10-mesh canvas 42 by 14 inches to obtain a piece of finished needlepoint about 39 by 11 inches.

Stitching Directions

To stitch the wall hanging, start at the top of your canvas. Begin at "A" on the graph and work to "B." Then work from "C" to "D." Repeat graph from "C" to "D" 4 times more for a total of 5 times. Stitch 2 rows of white. Work from "E" to "F." Repeat graph from "E" to "F" 2 times more for a total of 3 times. Then work from "G" to "H."

Color and Stitch Key

The colors in the color key are not those of the original blanket but my adaptation instead. Yarn numbers refer to Paterna yarns. The location and choice of stitches are indicated in the key. See color Plate 9.

Creative Alternatives

To restore the original colors to the hanging, change the brown Mosaic stitch areas to green (✳G28), the brown Basketweave stitch areas to red (✳240), and the flowers inside the diamonds to yellow (✳441). The black (✳050) and white (✳012) areas remain the same.

To change the stitches, use Parisian Variation II in place of the Mosaic stitch; use St. George and St. Andrew Cross stitch in place of Basketweave in all other brown areas; use Brick stitch for all white areas; and use Basketweave stitch or Continental stitch for all black areas.

To change the pattern of the wall hanging, cut and bind a piece of 10-mesh canvas 42 by 14 inches to obtain a piece of finished needlepoint about 38½ by 11 inches. Starting at the top of the canvas, stitch from "E" to "F." Repeat work from "E" to 'F" 6 times more. Then stitch from "G" to "H."

hopi kachina pillow

A Hopi kachina doll called Butterfly Maiden is the source for this design. For the Hopi Indians of northeastern Arizona, kachinas are spiritual beings who inhabit the high San Francisco Peaks of Arizona. The earthly representation of the kachina spirits are the thirty or so masked dancers who, during the Bean Dance in February and the Home Dance in July, distribute kachina dolls to the young girls. The design and symbolism of each kachina doll explains its ritual meaning within the polytheistic and animistic religion of the Hopi. Parents hang the kachina dolls on the wall of the Hopi dwelling to teach their children the complex spirit world of the more than 200 different kachinas.

Hopi men carve the kachina dolls from cottonwood roots, paint them with bright colors, and add the necessary costume details such as feathers. Kachina dolls have become very popular with collectors and, consequently, many—if not the majority—of kachina dolls made today, are for the non-Indian world.

Canvas

The pillow measures 212 by 184 threads. Cut and bind a piece of 14-mesh canvas 19 by 17 inches to obtain a piece of finished needlepoint about 15½ by 13½ inches.

Stitching Directions

Mark the center of the canvas with an indelible marker. Follow the arrows marked at the edges of the graph to find the starting point for the graph. This point corresponds to the center of the

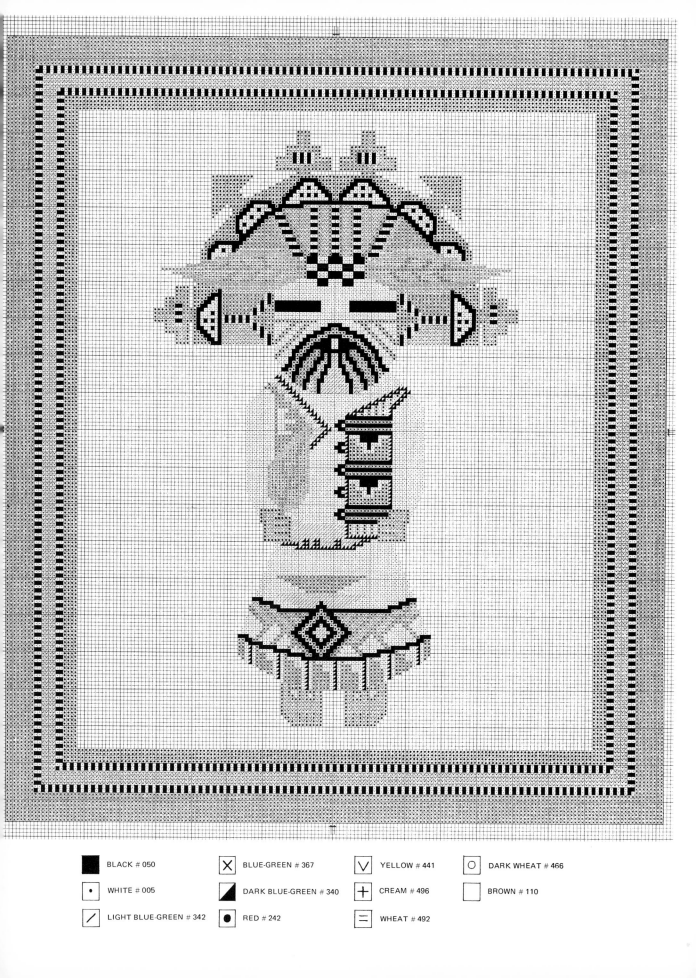

BLACK # 050

WHITE # 005

LIGHT BLUE-GREEN # 342

BLUE-GREEN # 367

DARK BLUE-GREEN # 340

RED # 242

YELLOW # 441

CREAM # 496

WHEAT # 492

DARK WHEAT # 466

BROWN # 110

canvas. Begin to stitch at the center of the canvas. Stitch the design first in Basketweave or Continental and then fill in the background with Scotch stitch over 4 meshes.

Color Key

The colors in the color key are those of the original kachina. Yarn numbers refer to Paterna yarns. See color Plate 8.

Creative Alternatives

To make the colors softer, change the blue-green to smoky blue, the red to rust, and the yellow to gold. The background could be steel gray, dark blue, or dark wheat.

To change the background stitch, try Oriental, Double Cross stitch or Smyrna Cross stitch. To use a decorative stitch for the blue-green, yellow, and red areas of the border, try St. George and St. Andrew Cross stitch.

To enlarge the pillow, use a piece of canvas 21 by 19 inches to obtain a piece of finished needlepoint about 18 by 15½ inches. Stitch on 12-mesh canvas.

For a slightly different pattern, omit the border and stitch the kachina and then the background as graphed. Use a piece of 10-mesh canvas 21 by 18 inches to obtain a piece of finished needlepoint about 17½ by 14½ inches.

Apache Basket Pillow

apache basket pillow

This design is adapted from a large Apache granary basket made by the White Mountain or San Carlos Apaches of eastern Arizona. The basket, made of willows, is of the coiled type.

The Apache women wrapped willow splints around a coil of one or more willows. As they built up the coils, the willow splint of one coil was secured in place by the coil below. Skilled weavers produced a variety of shapes—from flat plates to enormous jars.

The basket from which this design was taken is in a light color, while the figures are woven in a very dark color. The symbolism of Indian baskets is highly stylized and sometimes recognizable, but the meaning of the basket is often understood only by its maker. Frequently, the baskets combine obvious symbols with merely decorative motifs of the past which no longer carry any significance in themselves.

Canvas

The pillow measures 160 by 160 threads. Cut and bind a piece of 10-mesh canvas 19 inches square to obtain a piece of finished needlepoint 16 inches square.

Stitching Directions

Mark the center of the canvas with an indelible marker. Follow the arrows marked at the edges of the graph to find the starting point for the graph. This point corresponds to the center of the canvas. Begin to stitch at the center of the canvas. Stitch the design first in Basketweave or Continental and then fill in the background with Diagonal Parisian stitch.

<table>
<tr><td>☒</td><td>BROWN # 124
BASKETWEAVE OR CONTINENTAL STITCH</td><td>☐</td><td>WHEAT # 492
DIAGONAL PARISIAN STITCH</td></tr>
</table>

Color Key

The colors in the color key are very close to the original basket. Yarn numbers refer to Paterna yarns. See color Plate 4.

Creative Alternatives

You could reverse the two colors using wheat color for the figures and brown for the background. Other color combinations which would be effective include rust and cream; rust and green; or gray and gold.

To capture the texture of the basket, you could also use for the background Parisian stitch, Slanting Gobelin stitch, or Upright Gobelin stitch.

To convert the design into a belt, stitch several of the figures rearranged in a straight line on 16- or 18-mesh canvas. To convert it into a bellpull, stitch the figures horizontally on 10- or 12-mesh canvas.

To convert the design into a rug, stitch 8 squares. Vary the design from square to square. Add a brown border of several rows of Scotch stitch around each of the squares. Join the squares together to make a rug 2 squares wide and 4 squares long.

$\boxed{V}$ TURQUOISE SEED BEADS	$\boxed{X}$ BLACK SEED BEADS	$\boxed{\cdot}$ WHITE SEED BEADS	$\boxed{}$ WHITE # 005; PALE BLUE # 396

zuni jewelry purse

This beadwork design is adapted from a contemporary piece of Zuni silver jewelry with inlay of turquoise made in western New Mexico.

The Zuni Indians first began to work with silver in the 1870s. From the 1890s their work developed a distinctive character. Unlike the silver work of the Navajo, it emphasized the use of turquoise and other stones rather than the silver itself. The modern Zuni inlay technique joining stone and silver is built upon a much earlier tradition of attaching carved turquoise or shell to a wood or bone base by piñon pitch.

Canvas

The Zuni bird design measures 156 threads by 156 threads. Cut and bind a piece of 12-mesh canvas 16 inches square to obtain a finished piece of needlepoint 13 inches square.

Stitching Directions

Mark the center of the canvas with an indelible marker. Follow the arrows marked at the edges of the graph to find the starting point for the graph. This point corresponds to the center of the canvas. Begin to stitch at the center of the canvas. Bead the design and border first in Continental stitch and then work the background in St. George and St. Andrew Cross stitch.

117

Color Key

The colors are those of the original piece of jewelry. Yarn numbers refer to Paterna yarns. See color Plate 12.

Beading Directions

To bead this purse, you will need one 12-strand package each of turquoise, black, and white seed beads (see "Suppliers," p. 159); one skein of embroidery floss to match each bead color; beeswax and beading needles that are long and thin to fit through the holes of the beads.

To determine the correct mesh-size canvas for your beads, make a test swatch on 12-mesh canvas. If the beads cover the canvas, and if the stitched area remains flexible so that you can bend it back and forth, then you have found the correct size canvas for your beads. If the beads do not cover the canvas, try 14-mesh canvas instead of 12-mesh. If the stitched area is stiff and inflexible, try 10-mesh canvas instead of 12. Beads vary in size, depending on the supplier, so try them on a test piece first.

Thread the beading needle with one ply of embroidery floss. Double the thread and coat it with beeswax for strength. Use Continental stitch for bending. Secure the thread with two small stitches on the back. With the beading needle come up through the canvas, string one bead, and go back down through the canvas. The bead will sit on top of the canvas representing one stitch. Repeat this process for each stitch until you have covered the design and border. Then stitch the background with yarn in St. George and St. Andrew Cross stitch.

Instructions for finishing the purse, making a beaded fringe and the handle are on page 144 under "Finishing Your Project."

Creative Alternatives

Other colors would work well for this design. If you want to bead the purse, however, you will be limited by the colors available in seed beads.

Alternative stitches for the background could be the Cross stitch or the Small Chequer stitch. The background stitch should remain simple so that it does not detract from the beading.

To convert this purse design into a pillow, stitch the design on a piece of 10-mesh canvas 18 inches square to obtain a finished piece of needlepoint about 15½ inches square. Use the following colors of Paterna yarn in place of beads: black ⚡050; turquoise ⚡783; and white ⚡005.

Mimbres Pottery Pillow

mimbres pottery pillow

An ancient piece of pottery made by the Mimbres Indians in southwestern New Mexico about the thirteenth century was the inspiration for this design.

Mimbres pottery, despite its variations, followed a general pattern at that time. The bowls were usually black on white. In the center was an abstract representation of male figures, hunting scenes, or animals. The unusual charm of the Mimbres pottery comes from the combination of the central scene with finely executed panels of linework drawn below the rim of the bowl.

It is believed that men made the Mimbres pottery, although knowledge of Mimbres culture is meager. What is known is that the potters wheel was never used in prehistoric America and that pottery was built up from a free-hand base by coils of clay.

Canvas

The diameter of the pillow measures 170 threads. Cut and bind a piece of 12-mesh canvas 18 inches square to obtain a finished piece of needlepoint with a diameter of about 14½ inches.

Stitching Directions

Mark the center of the canvas with an indelible marker. Follow the arrows marked at the edges of the graph to find the starting point for the graph. This point corresponds to the center of the canvas. Begin to stitch at the center of the canvas. Stitch the design and border first and then fill in the background, all in Basketweave or Continental.

121

X BLACK # 108   • WHITE # 005   ☐ LIGHT GREY # 166

Color Key

The colors used are similar to those of the original pottery. Yarn numbers refer to Paterna yarns. See color Plate 10.

Creative Alternatives

To alter the colors and yet retain the authentic colors used in this type of pottery, change the black to dark rust ✳247; the gray to light rust ✳249; and the white to cream ✳496.

To change the stitch, use Mosaic stitch, Cashmere stitch, or Cross stitch in the white areas of the birds, and Moorish stitch in the light-gray background.

To convert this pillow into a rug, stitch the design on a piece of 5-mesh canvas 37 inches square to obtain a finished piece of needlepoint 34 inches in diameter.

X RUST # 247 • CREAM # 496 ☐ LIGHT RUST # 249

hohokam pottery pillow of mother and baby

This design is adapted from pottery made by the Hohokam Indians before the fifteenth century in southeastern Arizona.

The Hohokam Indians were excellent craftspersons not only in pottery but also in polished stone, mosaic, and carved shell ornaments. Among the Hohokam Indians, women made the pottery. They dug out the clay, cured it, built up their bowls by hand, and painted them with colors obtained from various plants. They fired their pottery by placing it in large stacks protected on all sides by large potsherds. They covered the stacks with fuel and left it to burn to coals.

Canvas

The pillow measures 172 by 172 threads. Cut and bind a piece of 12-mesh canvas 18 inches square to obtain a finished piece of needlepoint about 14½ inches square.

Stitching Directions

Mark the center of the canvas with an indelible marker. Follow the arrows marked at the edges of the graph to find the starting point for the graph. This point corresponds to the center of the canvas. Begin to stitch at the center of the canvas. Stitch the design first and then fill in the background. Work the design, background, and all but the cream-colored part of the border in Basketweave or Continental. Work the cream-colored part of the border in Scotch stitch over four.

Color Key

The colors are those of the original pottery. Yarn numbers refer to Paterna yarns. See color Plate 10.

Creative Alternatives

To alter the colors and yet retain the authentic colors used in this type of pottery, change the dark rust to black ✗108, the light rust to light gray ✗166, and the cream to white ✗005. As an alternative to this, you could stitch the figures in two shades of rust and use a cream color for the background.

To change the stitch, use St. George and St. Andrew Cross stitch, Brick stitch or Parisian stitch for the background. Use Smyrna stitch or Double Cross stitch for the cream-colored part of the border.

To convert this pillow into a pincushion, stitch only the two smaller figures on 18-mesh canvas, omitting the background, border, and the largest of the three figures. Create a new background by making a rectangle around the two figures measuring about 4½ by 5½ inches.

hohokam pottery pillow of bug

This design is also adapted from an ancient piece of Hohokam pottery made before the fifteenth century in southeastern Arizona.

Canvas

The diameter of the pillow measures 170 threads. Cut and bind a piece of 10-mesh canvas 20 inches square to obtain a finished piece of needlepoint 17 inches in diameter.

Stitching Directions

Mark the center of the canvas with an indelible marker. Follow the arrows marked at the edges of the graph to find the starting point for the graph. This point corresponds to the center of the canvas. Begin to stitch at the center of the canvas. The graph for the pillow represents half of the finished design. Stitch the graphed half and then repeat it in a mirror image to complete the design. Stitch the design and then fill in the background, all in Basketweave or Continental.

Color Key

The colors indicated are close to those of the original pottery. Yarn numbers refer to Paterna yarns. See color Plate 10.

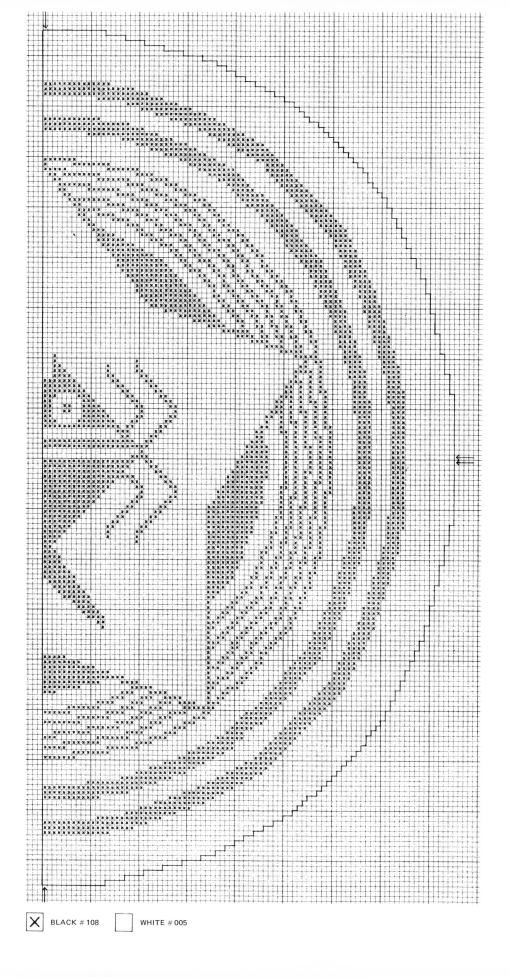

Hawaiian Quilt Pillow   *Plate 11*

Zuni Jewelry Purse,   Athabascan Beadwork Purse   Plate 12

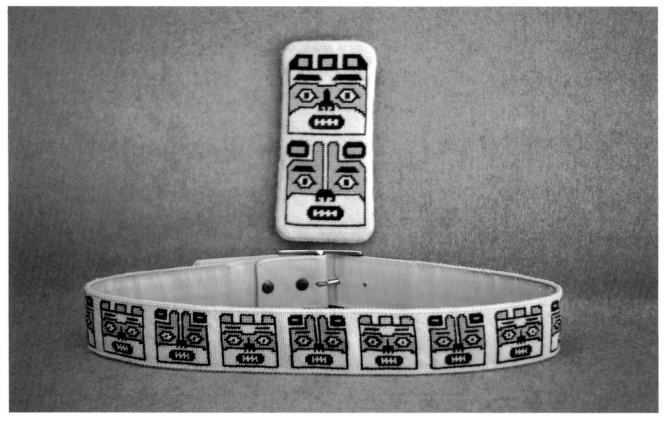

Chilkat Blanket Glasses Case,   Chilkat Blanket Belt   Plate 13

Chilkat Blanket Pillow

Plate 14

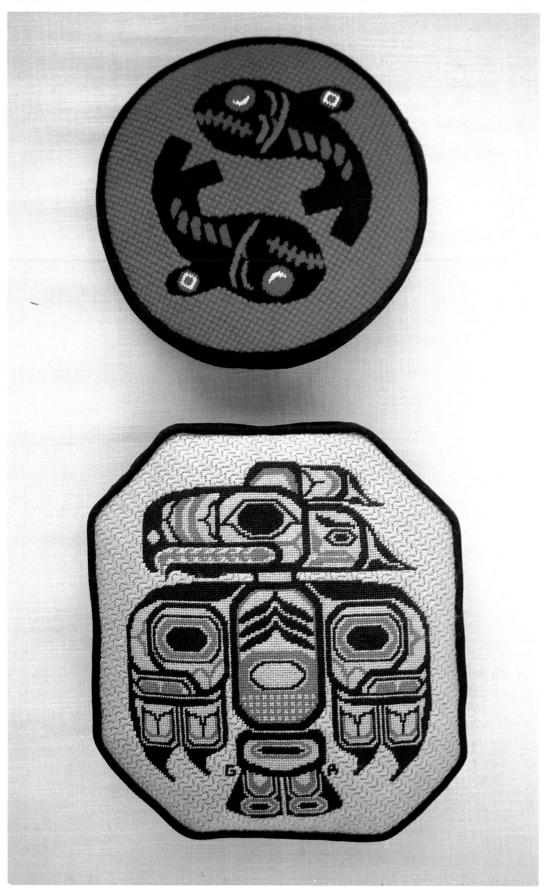

Above, Northwest Tribal Drum Pillow
Below, Tlingit Drum Pillow

Plate 15

adapting designs for needlepoint

Sources for Designs

The best source for tribal designs is the geographical area where such designs are still created as part of a living tradition. There you can see not only the making of the design but also its relation to the life of the people who use it. Unfortunately, very few such areas that have not been adversely affected by the growing commercial demand for tribal artifacts remain.

Another excellent source are the many collections specializing in the study and exhibition of tribal culture that are attached to universities or to natural history museums. Here you will find not only the designs but also the opinion of specialists concerning the origin of these designs and their relation to other tribal groups in the same area.

Of equal value are traveling collections of tribal culture. The better traveling exhibitions are usually furnished with detailed catalogues complete with photographs and historical and anthropological data. These catalogues are sometimes available in the bookshops of museums long after the traveling exhibition has gone. Specialized books concerning the artifacts and designs of various tribes are also available in museum and other bookshops as well.

Finally, you may discover after a little searching that you or a friend own some tribal artifacts or books that will furnish you with an excellent and convenient source for tribal designs.

132

designing your own

Athabascan Beadwork Purse

Creative Alternatives

To alter the colors and yet retain the authentic colors typical of this type of pottery, change the black and white to dark rust ✕247 and light rust ✕271, or to dark rust ✕247 and cream ✕496.

To change the stitch, use Mosaic stitch or Cross stitch for the background. Do not use a large or complicated stitch for the background as it will detract from the vibrant linework at the rim of the circle.

To convert this pillow design into a rug, stitch the design on a piece of 5-mesh canvas 37 inches square to obtain a finished piece of needlepoint about 34 inches in diameter.

Hohokam pottery from the collection of the Los Angeles County Museum of Natural History

Hohokam Pottery Pillow of Bug

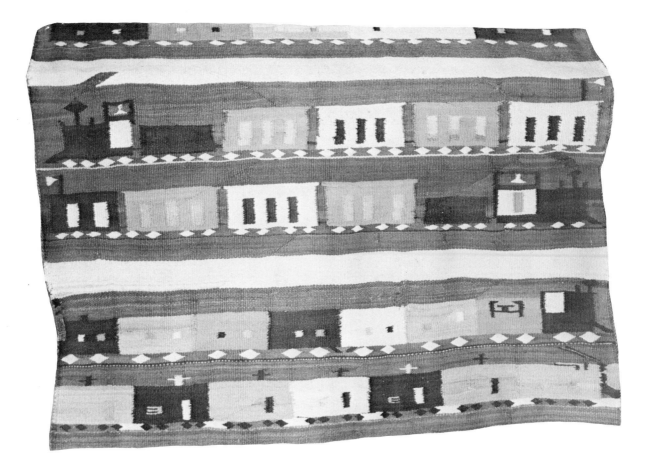

Design Detail and Canvas Size

There are a few points to keep in mind when you are adapting your own designs. Even simple designs are often too detailed to transfer directly to canvas. Your first task is to simplify the design by removing some of the detail. The goal is to eliminate unnecessary details and to enlarge the design sufficiently to make it easy to transfer to canvas and easy to stitch.

You will find that the amount of detail you can keep in a design depends on the overall size you want your project to be, and the mesh size of canvas you want to use. The larger the size of the project and the smaller the mesh size of the canvas, the more detail you can keep.

For an average size needlepoint project, such as a 15-inch-square pillow, 10-mesh canvas is appropriate for geometric designs or designs with simple bold curves. A slightly smaller size, 12-mesh canvas, allows more detail and produces curves with less of a rag-

Navajo pictorial rug from the collectionof the Los Angeles County Museum of Natural History

ged or saw-tooth edge. A still smaller size, 14-mesh canvas, will allow even finer details and smoother curves. The reason for this is simple: The smaller the canvas mesh, the more stitches per inch you have to indicate detail.

If you are working on a large project such as a rug or wall hanging, then you can use a larger mesh canvas for fine details and curves. An intricate design done on 18-mesh canvas for a pillow will show the detail equally well when enlarged for a rug on 10-mesh canvas. The reason for this is that a project 36 inches square on 10-mesh canvas contains approximately the same number of stitches as a project 20 inches square on 18-mesh canvas.

An easy way to determine which canvas mesh size is appropriate for your ungraphed design is to test all the sizes you think might work. Place each one separately on top of your drawing and then ask yourself when you have tested all the sizes which one seems to allow the amount of detail you wish to see in your finished needlepoint.

Navajo Rug Pillow of Train

transferring
a design
to canvas

There are two methods for transferring your design to canvas. One is suitable for freehand and free-flowing designs that are ungraphed and transferred directly to the canvas. The other method is suitable for geometric designs, repeat patterns, or designs with intricate details that are transferred to graph paper before being worked on canvas.

Ungraphed Designs

Sketch your design on a piece of newsprint or bond paper. Your drawing should be the same size as your finished piece of needlepoint. As you sketch, simplify your design by deleting details until the remaining details will fit on the canvas mesh size you wish to use. When you are satisfied with the size and balance of your design, draw a border around it. This border will mark the edge of your finished project. Now trace over the lines of your sketch with a black felt-tip pen to make them darker.

You are now ready to transfer your design directly to canvas. Mark the center of your drawing and then the center of your cut piece of canvas with a waterproof pen. Do not omit this step or your design may not be centered on your canvas. Now place your canvas on top of your design so that the center of the canvas is on top of the center of your design. Trace your design onto the canvas with a waterproof pen. The canvas is now ready for stitching— unless you want to paint it to show the location of colors. (See p. 139.)

(Note: if you do not have the confidence to attempt a freehand sketch of your design, take the design to a blueprinter and ask him to enlarge it to the size of your project. If the maximum size the blueprinter can make is smaller than your project, take the maximum size print obtainable and cut it into four equal parts. Then ask the blueprinter to enlarge each quarter to its maximum size. If this maximum size is still not large enough, cut each new section into quarters, and repeat the process. When the sections finally reach the necessary size, put them together with cellophane tape.)

Graphed Designs

This method for transferring a design to canvas requires the use of graph paper. You may use any size of graph paper, but large sheets are less cumbersome because you do not have to paste them together for most projects. I prefer graph paper with 10 or 12 squares to the inch as these sizes are more readily available in larger sheets than are others.

If your finished project must be a certain size, make an outline of that size on your canvas with a waterproof pen. Then count the number of canvas threads within this outline from top to bottom and from side to side. Next, count the same number of squares on the graph paper from top to bottom and from side to side and draw an outline around the squares.

The graph outline may be larger or smaller than your canvas outline, but that is not important. What is important is that the number of *canvas threads* and the number of *graph squares* within the outlined areas are the same. Each graph square will, consequently, represent one needlepoint stitch.

Now sketch your design within the outline on your graph paper. Work on your design until it is simplified and balanced to your satisfaction. (If you want to avoid freehand sketching, take your design to a blueprinter and have him enlarge the design to the size of the graph paper outline. You can then trace the design onto the graph paper.) Next, block in your design on the graph paper by tracing with a pen those squares adjacent to your sketch.

For mirror-image designs, you need to graph only half of the design as the mirror image simply repeats in reverse the first half.

For repeat patterns, you need to graph only the first pattern because it will serve as a model for the others.

Now find and mark the exact center of your graphed design. Then find and mark the exact center of your canvas with a waterproof pen. You are now ready to begin stitching. Count off the squares of your design on the graph and stitch each corresponding mesh of the canvas.

If you want to avoid counting while stitching, mark your canvas in advance. Count off the squares of your design from the center of the graph and mark each corresponding mesh of the canvas with a waterproof pen to designate different colors.

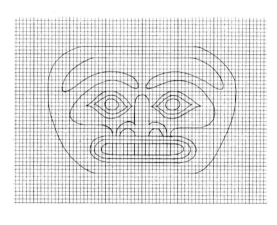

Design traced onto graph paper

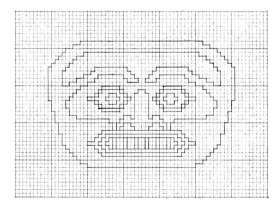

Design blocked in

138

Painting the Canvas

After your design is marked on the canvas, you may want to paint the design. Painting is not necessary, but indications where each color goes make it unnecessary to carry a color chart. Moreover, your yarn will always have the same color beneath it which will prevent flecks of light canvas from showing through your stitching.

Several types of paints are available for painting needlepoint canvas, including acrylic paints, oil paints, textile paints, and felt-tipped pens. Whatever type you choose *must* be waterproof. Oil paints must be thinned with turpentine and are slow to dry. Many textile paints have a strong odor and the canvas often needs ironing to make the paints waterproof. Felt-tipped pens do not provide vivid colors on canvas and their colors cannot be mixed.

Acrylic paints, by contrast, seem to have few disadvantages. They are definitely waterproof once dry, easily mixed, thinned with water, and quick drying. I use an acrylic extender with water to thin the paint. This spreads the paint on the canvas more evenly and the color dries with a more vivid hue.

Painting needlepoint canvases is a continual learning process. From my experience I have found it helpful to color the preliminary sketch on paper before painting the canvas. This helps me to decide on the location of colors before painting the canvas. If you make a mistake in painting the canvas, you can paint it out by using paint to match the color of the canvas.

Difficulty in spreading paint on canvas can usually be overcome by thinning the paint to a workable consistency. It should not be so thick that it clogs the canvas holes or so thin that it soaks through to the other side of the canvas. There is no exact formula. I recommend that you begin by thinning the paint to the consistency of heavy cream. You can adjust from there. You should remember, when mixing your paints, that the color will dry darker and duller on canvas than on your wet palette.

finishing your project

Professional Finishing and Blocking

I usually recommend professional blocking and finishing for most needlepoint projects. Needlepoint is time consuming and, if you have done a careful job of stitching, your work deserves careful finishing. It is best, however, to check the reputation of the finisher before you turn over your work. Look at several other projects the finisher has done and decide whether the work is the quality you want.

When I do a project that is not a conventional shape, I find it helpful, before I begin, to talk to the finisher who can then assist me with the pattern layout. This avoids any unexpected difficulties when the project is completed and goes to the finisher.

If a project is to have a backing, such as a pillow or a wall hanging, I select my own fabric for the backing rather than leave the choice to the finisher. This way I can be certain that the color and texture are exactly what I want. Finishers often supply velvet or velveteen, but I usually avoid these fabrics because they are so common. There are many more interesting textures and patterns available in wool, cotton, and linen to enhance your finished needlepoint.

Blocking Your Own Project

Should you decide to block your own needlepoint, the method below works well and should smooth and set the yarn and restore the original shape to your canvas. You will need the following supplies: a board, such as plywood, larger than your needlepoint piece; brass brads or stainless steel T pins; a hammer; a T square; brown wrapping paper approximately the size of the board; and a waterproof pen.

Step 1: Measure the size your finished work is to be and draw an outline on the wrapping paper with a waterproof pen. It helps to make an outline of your needlepoint piece for blocking purposes *before* you begin stitching. Use the T square to make all corners of the outline perfectly square. Now secure the paper on top of the plywood.

Step 2: Wrap your dry needlepoint piece in a lukewarm, wet bath towel and leave it for several hours to dampen but not soak.

Step 3: Remove the needlepoint from the towel and tack it face up with brass brads or stainless steel T pins on top of the brown paper so that the stitched design conforms to the drawn outline. You should tack the canvas all the way around at half-inch or inch intervals. Leave the canvas tacked to the board until it is completely dry—which may take from 24 to 48 hours.

Finishing Your Own Project

If you decide to do your own finishing, a knife-edge pillow without welting is the simplest of all pillows to do. You will need the following supplies: fabric to back your pillow; needle and thread; scissors; straight pins; sewing machine; and filling for the pillow.

Step 1: After you have blocked your needlepoint piece, set your sewing machine for a fine zigzag stitch and sew around your needlepoint piece on the canvas just outside your stitching. Trim the excess canvas leaving a half inch of canvas outside your stitching.

Step 2: Cut the backing fabric to match the size of your needlepoint stitching plus the half inch of canvas. Pin the right side of the fabric to the right side of your needlepoint piece.

Step 3: With the wrong side of your needlepoint piece facing up, sew the backing to the needlepoint. Sew into one row of your needlepoint stitching. Do not sew all four sides closed. Leave an opening at the bottom of the pillow large enough to turn your pillow inside out.

Step 4: Turn your pillow inside out so that the right sides are facing out. Stuff the pillow firmly with filling. Turn under the seams of the open area and hand stitch the flap closed.

Making Tassels

Tassels make effective accents for many needlepoint items, particularly for knife-edge pillows. The following directions are for a tassel with a decorative webbing around its head. Examples of this type can be seen on pages 2, 24, 44, and 146.

The average tassel will take about two ounces of yarn. Do not skimp on the amount of yarn you use, as tassels accent pillows best when the tassels are large and full. In each tassel try blending several yarn textures and colors. The webbing for the tassel is often more effective when it is done in a contrasting color to the tassel.

To make tassels you will need the following supplies: a piece of cardboard cut slightly longer than the desired length of your tassel; yarn; a long strand of contrasting yarn for the webbing; and a tapestry needle.

Step 1: Starting at one end, wrap the yarn repeatedly around the piece of cardboard. When all the yarn is wrapped around the cardboard, slip a separate strand of yarn under the wrapped yarn (A) and tie the separate strand tightly and securely (B). At the opposite end of the cardboard, cut through all the strands of yarn. You now have strands of yarn hanging from a knot at the top (C).

Step 2: Form the tassel head by tying another strand of yarn around the tassel about one third of the distance from the top of the tassel. Next, tie the strand of yarn for the webbing around the tassel at the base of the head. Leave one side as long as possible and thread this long side with a needle (D). You are now ready to webb the tassel head.

Step 3: With the threaded strand of yarn, make loose loops around the base of the tassel head (E). When you have made loops all the way around the base, begin row two of the webbing by catching the top of the first loop with your needle and making a second loop (F). Continue working around the tassel, forming new loops until the whole tassel head is covered with the webbing

(G). When you reach the top of the tassel, end the yarn by taking three little stitches, one on top of another, and then pull the needle through the tassel head from the top to the base. Cut off the yarn at the base of the tassel and plump the tassel to hide the cut end.

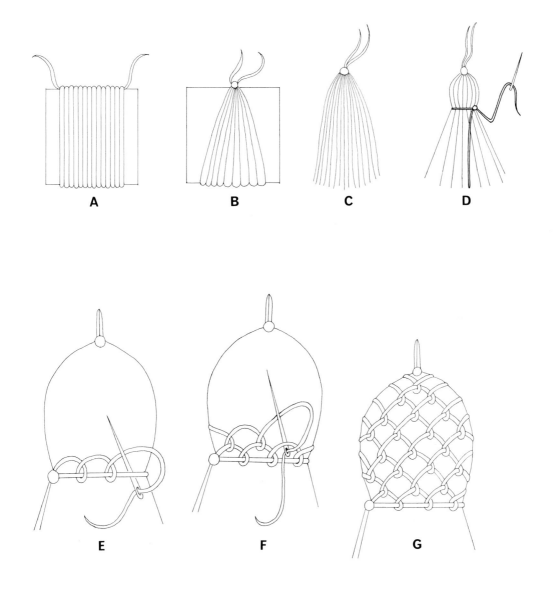

A   B   C   D

E   F   G

Finishing a Beaded Purse

Finishing a beaded purse is only slightly more difficult than making a knife-edge pillow. You will need the following supplies for each purse: fabric to back your needlepoint and to line the purse; needle and thread; scissors; straight pins; sewing machine; beading needles; and several packages of 12-strand strung seed beads.

Step 1: After you have blocked your needlepoint piece, set your sewing machine for a fine zigzag stitch and sew around your needlepoint piece just outside your stitching. Trim the excess canvas leaving a half inch of canvas outside your stitching.

Step 2: Cut the backing fabric to match the size of your needlepoint stitching plus the half inch of canvas. Cut two pieces of lining to match the size of the backing. Set the lining pieces aside for now.

Step 3: Pin the right side of the backing fabric to the right side of the needlepoint piece. With the wrong side of the needlepoint piece facing up, sew the backing fabric to the needlepoint on three sides, leaving the top side open. Turn the purse inside out so that the right sides are now facing out.

Step 4: Thread a beading needle with polyester sewing thread and secure the thread to the inside of the purse at the top of one side. Sew through the seam from the inside to the outside. String about four inches of beads onto the thread and make a loop of the beads by pushing the needle to the inside seam of the purse. Secure the thread to the inside of the purse. Repeat this process until you have made a fringe of beads along the sides and the bottom of the purse.

Step 5: Leaving a half-inch seam, machine stitch the two pieces of lining right sides together on three sides with the top side left open. Do *not* turn the lining inside out. Tack it at the bottom corners to the inside of the purse. Turn under the top seams of the lining and the purse, and then blind stitch the lining to the purse along the top.

Step 6: Sew one ring to each top corner of the purse. Using

macramé cord, make a handle of square knots and tie one end of the handle to one ring, the other end of the handle to the other ring. Center and sew the small button to the top of the back of the purse. On the top of the front center of the purse, sew a thread loop to fit over the button. This will close the purse.

Marquesas Islands Carved Coconut

appendix

glossary of stitches

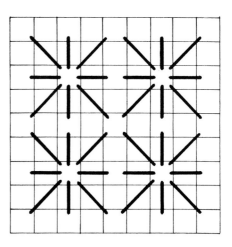

Algerian Eye Stitch
(*also known as Star Stitch*)

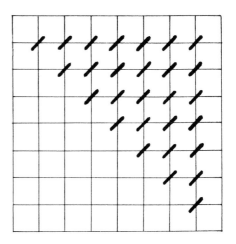

Basketweave Stitch
(*also known as Diagonal Tent Stitch*)

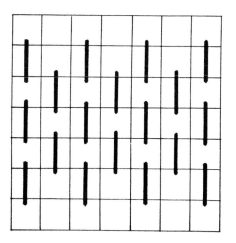

Brick Stitch

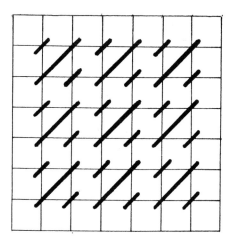

Cashmere Stitch

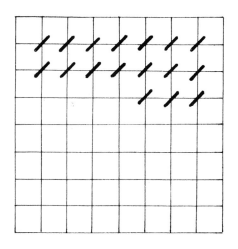

Continental Stitch
(also known as Tent Stitch)

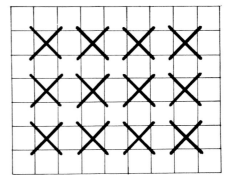

Cross Stitch

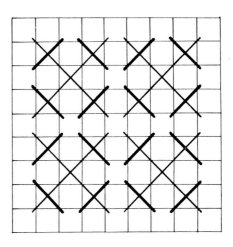

Crossed Corners Stitch
(also known as Rice Stitch and
William and Mary Stitch)

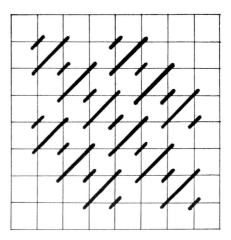

Diagonal Mosaic Stitch

150

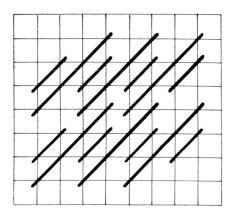

Diagonal Parisian Stitch

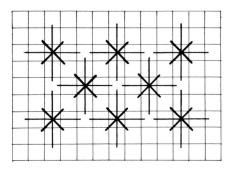

Double Cross Stitch

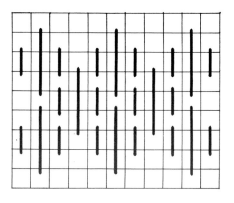

Hungarian Stitch

151

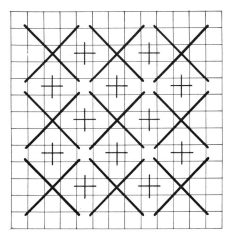

Large and Upright Cross Stitch

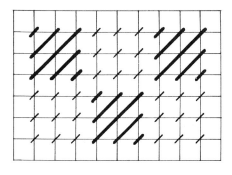

Large Chequer Stitch (over 3 meshes)

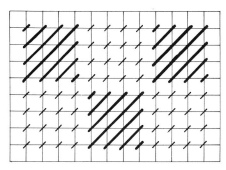

Large Chequer Stitch (over 4 meshes)

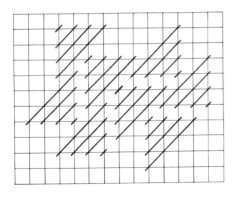

Milanese Stitch

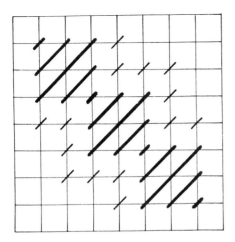

Moorish Stitch

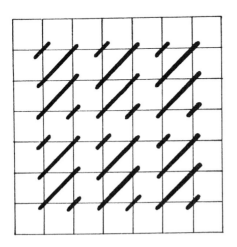

Mosaic Stitch

153

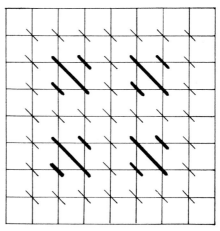

Mosaic Stitch Variation

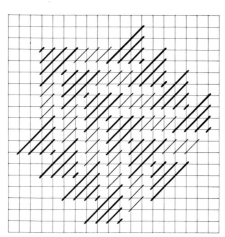

Oriental Stitch

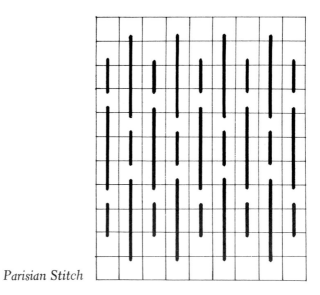

Parisian Stitch

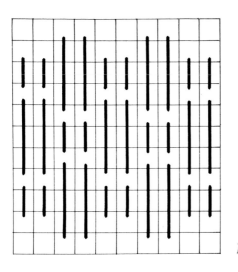

Parisian Stitch, Variation I

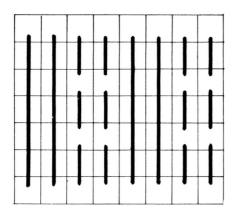

Parisian Stitch, Variation II

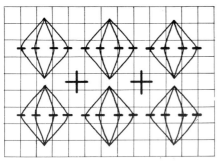

Rococo Stitch, Variation

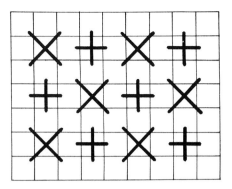

St. George and St. Andrew Cross Stitch

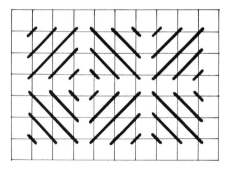

*Scotch Stitch (over 3 meshes—
also known as Cushion Stitch
and Flat Stitch)*

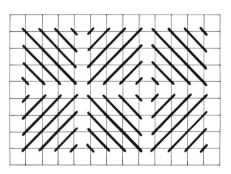

*Scotch Stitch (over 4 meshes—
also known as Cushion Stitch
and Flat Stitch)*

156

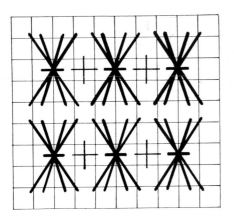

Shell Stitch (also known as Sheaf Stitch)

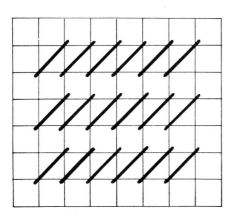

Slanting Gobelin Stitch

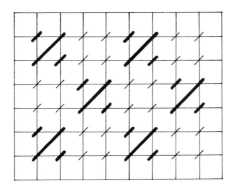

Small Chequer Stitch

157

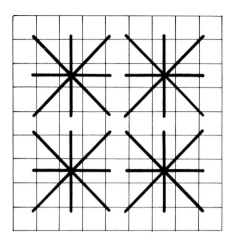

*Smyrna Cross **Stitch***

Upright Gobelin Stitch
(also known as Straight Gobelin Stitch
and Gobelin Droit Stitch)

suppliers

YARNS:

Paternayan Bros. Inc.
312 East 95th Street
New York, New York 10028

Nantucket Needleworks
11 South Water Street
Nantucket, Massachusetts 02554

STRUNG SEED BEADS:

Hazel Pearson Handicrafts
4128 Temple City Boulevard
Rosemead, California 91770